MON

3-97

17
-6-97
3-97

know
your rights

by Lewis Katz

illustrations by Tom Shephard

Traffic Stops

Personal Information Access

Choosing a Lawyer · **Airport Luggage Searches**

Human Services Home Visits · **Building Code Inspections**

Warrantless Searches · **Disclosures on Job Applications**

Campus Regulation Enforcement · **Bad Credit Repair** · **Arrest**

Booking · **Who to Call** · **Making Bail** · **While Waiting for Bail**

False ID's · **Domestic Violence** · **Eviction** · **Using Credit Cards**

Towed Cars/Automobile Impoundment · **Wrongful Discharge**

Landlord Searches · **Abortion** · **Checking Your Credit Rating**

Police Questioning of Travelers · **Prosecuting Date Rape**

Release of Student Records · **High School Locker Searches**

Pat-downs at Concerts · **Student Pranks** · **Sealing Arrest Records**

Police Visits to Loud Parties · **Witholding Enough Taxes**

HIV Testing · **Police Interrogation** · **Privacy Rights in the Home**

College Disciplinary Proceedings · **Drug Testing** · **Sexual Harassment**

Automobile Searches · **Establishing Credit** · **Telephone Harassment**

Sobriety Checkpoints · **Automobile Accidents** · **Dormitory Searches**

Taxation of Tuition Benefits · **Airport Security Checks**

For information, please call or write:

Banks-Baldwin Law Publishing Company
University Center
P.O. Box 1974
Cleveland, Ohio 44106

216/721-7373
FAX 216/721-8055

ISBN 0-8322-0450-1

ACKNOWLEDGMENTS

My thanks to Tyler, Adam, Brett, and Mark for their helpful suggestions and for making this book necessary. Thanks also to Russell Wood, my research assistant, for his invaluable assistance in researching the law on many of these issues.

Thanks especially to Jan Karen Katz, my wife, editor, keeper of the better judgment, and my best friend, for efforts on this manuscript and everything that has been good about my life since 1963.

CONTENTS

Chapter | Page

1   Your Rights: Use Them or Lose Them ...   1

2   In Your Car   7

    Flashing lights in the rearview mirror   7
    "License and registration, please"   13
    Searching your car   17
    Towing your car   22
    Under the influence of drugs or alcohol   24
    Sobriety checkpoints   27
    Accidents   30

3   When Traveling   35

    Airport security checkpoints   36
    Airport luggage searches   38
    Stopped by airport security   42
    Using someone else's airline ticket   45
    Traveling by bus   47

4   In Your Home   53

    Is Big Brother really watching?   54
    The police are at the door   55
    Consent to search given by another   57
    Searching with or without a warrant   60
    Noisy parties and fights   63
    Domestic disputes   67
    Entry by building inspectors and other
      government officials   70
    Landlords and eviction   73

5   On Campus   77

    Dorm room searches   77
    Disciplinary hearings   83
    In trouble off campus   86
    Flunking out   90
    Dealing with campus police   91
    Mandatory drug testing   95
    Privacy of student records   96
    Sexual harassment   97

Chapter   Page

Obscene telephone callers and other harassers   99
Campus crime   102
Date rape   104
Reporting sexual assault   106
HIV testing and privacy   107

6   What? You've Been Arrested?   111

Arrest procedures   111
Bail   113
One phone call   115
Miranda rights   117
Remaining silent   118
Getting a lawyer   122
Going to jail   126
Don't panic!   127

7   On Taxes   129

8   About Credit   133

9   On The Job   141

10   Abortion   149

Index   153

1 YOUR RIGHTS: USE THEM OR LOSE THEM

This book had its origins in a Greyhound Bus terminal a quarter of a century ago. It was during the Viet Nam War, and Detroit was a port of exit for young Americans escaping the draft into Canada. I was in Detroit at an annual law schools' convention and was returning to my family in Cleveland, where I was an assistant professor of law. I was not a draft dodger; in fact, at the time, I was an officer in the Navy Reserves. However, I did not look entirely unlike the young men involved in avoiding the draft. My hair was long and I had a mustache and beard.

It was Christmastime and authorities were braced for the return of some of those who had fled to Canada returning to the country to visit with their families for the holidays. As I headed for the bus to Cleveland, I was approached by a man in street clothes who flashed a badge and identified himself as an agent of the Immigration and Naturalization Service. In as menacing a tone as one might have expected at a border checkpoint in Berlin, this government agent started asking me questions. He asked me where I was going, and I responded, "Cleveland." Then he asked to see my driver's license and draft card.

All at once it struck me that I was responding just as he expected me to: I was nervous and obliging his requests for information. Suddenly, I understood how it is that most people answer any question put to them by a police officer or other person with a badge of authority, regardless of the consequences. How could I react the same way? I knew my rights and the limits of the INS agent's authority. I realized that I had to refuse further requests from this officer. He wasn't polite; he used a tone of voice which he expected would produce the information he sought. If I didn't stand up to him, how could I ever expect anyone else to do so?

I wondered how someone not knowledgeable about the law could know under similar circumstances that she need not comply with official requests for information. He was shocked when I told him that I would not show him my driver's license or draft card. He repeated his request, which sounded more and more like a demand, and I maintained my refusal. I told him that he had no authority to do more than ask. I also said that I had no intention of complying unless he forced me to and that he would regret using that force.

At that, I turned away and walked the few yards to the bus entrance, wondering if he was going to let me climb on to the bus or whether he would grab me and illegally use force to see my identification. I made it to the bus and took a seat mid-way back. My adversary walked along the bus and stood outside, staring at me through the window, as though he was about to come inside and drag me off the bus. He didn't, and finally the bus left.

Throughout this encounter, I was frightened, even though I knew he had no authority to force me to comply with his requests, and even though I knew I had nothing to hide. But police aren't the only authorities we run into on a daily basis. A guide is needed for all these encounters. I decided then and there to write a book about how to behave when confronted with such a situation.

Since that encounter, legal intimidation has not gotten better. It has gotten worse. In the name of the "war on drugs," our government is doing things we once thought only other governments do. Police and other officials in this country intercept innocent people every day and force them to prove their innocence, sometimes illegally searching them and their automobiles. The only time we hear about these encounters in the newspapers or on television is when drugs are discovered. We don't hear about how many people are stopped when no drugs are found.

In most of these encounters, the police do not have suspicion or probable cause, the legal standards governing investigative stops and arrests, and they lack authority to force compliance with their requests. Nonetheless, their requests sound like commands. Yet, when a violation of the law is discovered, and a case gets to court, the police describe what happened as though the defendant had consented to the search. In other words, *the person searched did not have to consent.*

We once looked to the United States Supreme Court to protect the rights of individuals. Now, that Court has enlisted foursquare in the war on drugs. It has aided the development of the myth that people who don't know they have the right to refuse to cooperate have nevertheless voluntarily cooperated with aggressive police officers and consented to these searches.

Hence, the need for this book is greater now than when it was first conceived. The law will not protect your right to be left alone unless you know you have that right and assert it when it is challenged. That knowledge can save you from a lot of unnecessary trouble.

A lawyer friend of mine told me that his son, a recent college graduate, was traveling in the Southwest and was stopped for speeding on an Oklahoma interstate. The young man sported a shaved head and two earrings in an earlobe. Nonetheless, the officer was courteous and businesslike. After writing up the ticket, the officer politely asked the young man to get out of his car and then asked if he could search the car. Following a very slight pause, my friend's son consented to the search of his car.

He then stood by helplessly as the officer and his partner very thoroughly searched the car, the trunk, and all of the young man's possessions. On the bottom of a zippered compartment of a backpack, underneath socks and underwear, one of the officers found a ziplocked plastic baggy containing a minute quantity of marijuana. The father learned of this when he received a call from his son, who was in a suburban Oklahoma jail.

My conversation with the father the following day was another reason which prompted me to write this book. Like many parents, his telephone conversation with his son contained a fair amount of "I-told-you-so"s. The father said he asked his son if he hadn't told him many times not to carry drugs around in the car, if he insisted on having drugs at all. Naturally, he moaned when his son responded that, since it was such a small amount, he didn't think it would be a problem.

Since he had given his son all this good advice, I asked the lawyer if he had ever advised his son not to consent to a search. He paused, and then smiled and admitted he had not. He did say, however, that he asked his son why he consented to the search. The young man responded, "How could I say no to a highway patrol officer?"

Of course he could have said *no*. If the officer had the legal authority to search the car, he would not have asked in the first place; he would have just searched the car. Thus, when dealing with police or other government officials, you need to know when and how to assert your rights. In this book I will tell you just that, by exploring those situations where you are most likely to come into contact with police and other governmental authorities. More importantly, I will tell you how to react, and how to pursue your rights after the encounter. This guidance will go beyond encounters with police and will cover a variety of other situations, such as questions arising from encounters with building and welfare inspectors, and will cover other topics such as eviction, taxes, employment issues, drug testing, and college disciplinary proceedings.

Understand that not every police officer you meet will be unfair. You have the right to turn to police for help, and you don't forfeit that right by asserting other rights. Nonetheless, in the situations which I will discuss, the officer will seek information which could damage you. Yet there are different ways of going about that. Most police officers are professionals, not power hungry oppressors out to gain the upper hand over every person with whom they come in contact.

But there *is* the other type of cop. Every police officer, during a relaxed conversation, will acknowledge the existence of bad cops, the curse of the good cop's existence. Newspapers are not filled with reports of standard traffic stops by courteous police officers who issue warnings or tickets and then send motorists on their way after a brief interval. (Why should those stories be in the newspaper? We have the right to expect that behavior from public servants.) The newspapers do report, however, incidents which deviate from the acceptable pattern. And no one who was old enough to watch television in 1991 will ever forget the images captured on videocam of rogue (regardless of what the first jury said) cops in Los Angeles mercilessly beating Rodney King. Every professional police officer now must live down that image, and it isn't easy.

Encounters with abusive cops are upsetting, even though most are not likely to subject a citizen to a roadside beating. Such a cop intimidates and misuses authority at least partially to scare the victim. Police departments have not done all they should to weed out these officers.

It is imperative that you recall all details of an experience with a police officer that is out of the ordinary, not just the one which you might have with an abusive cop. Your protection or ultimate vindication rests on your ability to recreate the scene. Hopefully, someone is with you who can verify the details, but even if you are alone, your ability to recall exactly what is done and (equally important) what is *said* is crucial.

Write a narrative of the encounter as soon as possible after it ends and pay attention to detail, especially the precise words the officer uses. Your recollection becomes more important later, if the encounter involves a search of you or your car or if it leads to any additional charges, other than the traffic citation which may be the original reason for the stop.

But even if the incident does not lead to more serious consequences, if you believe the police officer's behavior is inappropriate, make sure you write down an accurate record of your encounter. Certainly, if the officer's behavior seems out of line, if the officer's manner is discourteous, if the officer's language is offensive, consider reporting it. If the officer makes sexual overtures to you or suggests meeting or dating at a later time, that behavior is unacceptable not only to you, but also to the police department and to the local governmental unit. Don't ignore it. The more that citizens complain about such behavior, the more police departments will see to it that such behavior is not tolerated.

Any position of authority can be and has been abused, whether that of school administrator or landlord. Keep records of meetings and phone conversations. A clear and organized presentation of your side of the story will make it much easier to assert and vindicate your rights.

Ultimately, your best bet is to be informed: to know what to expect and how to respond. Let's try to explore some common situations. There is no way to anticipate every question or situation, but if you understand the norm, you are more likely to be able to handle even the unusual.

2 IN YOUR CAR

If you are a typical American, most of your contacts with police result from driving your car or from reporting it stolen. Your views about the police are shaped largely by the nature of these experiences. These encounters can take many forms depending on the reason for the stop, the ensuing behavior of the officer, and you, the motorist. Often, it is *your* behavior that determines how it goes.

Flashing lights in the rearview mirror

May a police officer stop my car just because she feels like it?

No. The officer must see, and be able to describe, specific facts that give her a reasonable basis to suspect that you have broken a traffic law, such as speeding or running a red light, or that you are committing some more serious offense, such as drunk driving. Legally, the officer may not stop you randomly or on a hunch that you are doing something wrong. She may not stop you because she doesn't like your looks or hair. Certainly, your race is not a valid reason for stopping your car. Nor is a Grateful Dead sticker in a car window sufficient grounds for a lawful stop, regardless of what the officer may think the sticker signifies.

In reality, we know that such illegal stops occur. People are sometimes stopped, illegally, because the officer spots a young driver in a fancy car and wonders how he came to drive such a car. If an illegal stop leads to the discovery of evidence of a crime, that evidence should ultimately be suppressed in court because its discovery resulted from an illegal stop. Note, however, that an officer who engages in such illegal conduct may not be above perjuring herself in court and claiming that she stopped the car because of a traffic violation, rather than the looks, age, or race of the driver. However, let's not assume the worst because the worst is an exception, not the usual situation.

When I see red lights in my rear view mirror I get nervous— how should I respond?

Every motorist who has looked in a rear view mirror and seen police lights flashing has had a momentary urge to take off. Don't. First, there may be several harmless reasons for the flashing lights. The police car may be responding to an emergency call, and your failure to pull over may delay the response or block the way for fire engines or ambulances that may follow the police, endangering people who need help. This could result in your receiving an expensive ticket. Also, the officer may be after another motorist, not you. The flashing lights are a signal to everyone to move to the right and allow the officer to pass.

However, it is just as likely that the police car's ominous flashing lights are a signal for you to pull over. It's natural to experience that sick feeling in the pit of your stomach, but you can eliminate those visions of yourself in prison pinstripes. In almost every instance, you are being stopped for a simple traffic violation which does not even allow for your arrest, let alone a jail sentence. *It's important for you to understand at that moment that even if you have been speeding or have committed a similar traffic offense you are not a criminal, and society expects the police officer to refrain from treating you like one.*

Attempting to flee from or elude the officer, however, is a serious, and possibly dangerous, offense. Even if you think the officer has no legal reason for stopping you, pull over. The time for challenging the stop is later, in court. Don't get into a legal argument with the officer; you may say things impulsively which can later be used against you.

Although you are nervous, try to relax and stay calm; take a deep breath. You are an American and have rights which are about to kick in and, if you use your head, those rights will limit your contact with the officer and keep you from getting into more serious trouble. In the following pages, we will discuss just what the officer may do following this stop, and we will explore your rights and, more importantly, show you how to use them to your advantage.

What initial steps should I take in dealing with the officer?

A word of caution is in order. Just because you know your rights and the limits the law places on the police officer, do not act rudely or crudely. Most police officers are professionals who act in a business-like manner and abide by the law. They are also human beings, likely to respond in kind to an offensive or obnoxious motorist, writing you tickets for every possible violation. Even worse, you might mouth off to a rogue cop and endanger yourself or at least subject yourself to an unnecessarily prolonged encounter or even a trip to the police station.

Mentally note exactly what has happened, including the officer's and your behavior and the surrounding circumstances. Write it down as soon afterward as possible. It will help you to reconstruct what happened if you later have to tell a lawyer or judge.

Quite often highways are patrolled by plainclothes traffic officers, whose effectiveness rests on our natural tendency to slow down and carefully observe the rules of traffic when we see a marked police car but to behave normally when the car next to us does not appear to be a police car.

However, be aware that there are reports of motorists being victimized by persons pretending to be plainclothes officers. If you are ordered over on a highway by an unmarked car, raise your windows and lock the door. Don't unlock the door or lower your window until the person approaching your car shows you a badge or police identification. No legitimate law enforcement officer would engage you in this setting without proper ID and a willingness to show it to you. If the officer promises to show you the identification after you walk back to his car with him, insist that he produce it first. If the officer tells you that he does not have his identification with him, insist that he radio for a uniformed patrol officer before you will roll down the window or unlock the car. Your life could depend on your caution.

Should I get out of my car as soon as I am pulled over and approach the police car before the officer approaches me?

No, stay where you are. This isn't a social call, and there is an established protocol for the officer to follow. First and foremost in the officer's mind at the moment is his safety. Even though you know that you are no threat, he doesn't know that yet. The officer has the right to engage you in ways, *within limits*, that minimize any potential danger to himself. Your safety is an issue as well. Getting pulled over is likely to distract you from focusing as clearly as you should on safety concerns. Jumping out of your car and approaching the police car may place you in danger from passing traffic.

This conduct may also make the officer unnecessarily suspicious, instead of demonstrating your friendliness and cooperativeness. The officer may be concerned that being stopped has made you angry and that you are approaching the police car to express that anger. In addition, if the officer is seated and you are standing outside the police car, he may be rightfully concerned that your physical position gives you the edge. At the very least, your effort at cooperation may make him suspicious that you want to keep him away from your car and from looking into your car window because you have something to hide.

So stay where you are and let the police officer take the lead. Use the time while you wait for the officer to compose yourself and sort out what is happening. Remember your rights and strengthen your resolve not to let the situation get worse than it is. A traffic ticket will likely complicate your life, but keep in mind it is a minor complication.

All right, I didn't jump out, but now I am sitting here waiting for the officer to come up to me. Why is he making me wait?

While you are imagining dire possibilities, there is a very simple explanation for the delay. The officer has to notify his command that he is momentarily unavailable for calls and about to leave the car. He is probably also checking your license plate through the computer network to establish that the car has not been reported stolen and that the car you are driving matches the one for which the plate was issued.

Once the officer approaches my car, may he order me out?

Yes, the officer may order you and any other occupants out of the car. Once you are out, he may order you back into the car or into the police cruiser. Although this sounds rather silly, police officers have the power to take the steps they think necessary to ensure their safety. The officer needs no additional justification other than a lawful stop to order you out or to order you to remain inside your car. It is within his discretion to determine whether he will be safer with you inside or outside of your car.

If the officer orders me out of the car, may he then search me or the car?

At this stage of the traffic stop, ordering you from the car is the full extent of the officer's power. Without additional facts indicating that you are dangerous or guilty of a more serious offense, the officer may not search you or your car. Once you are out of the car, if the officer sees a bulge in your clothing which could be a weapon or if your conduct otherwise makes the officer think you may be carrying a weapon, he may conduct a pat-down search of your outer clothing to make sure that you don't have a weapon. The officer may not reach inside your pockets or under your outer clothing, unless during the pat-down he feels an object which could be a weapon.

If he finds a weapon, you are in serious trouble. Naturally, while the car door is opened so that you can exit at the officer's command, he may see a weapon or other incriminating objects in open sight. Seeing objects in open sight or plain view while the car door is open means just that. It does not mean reaching under the seat, looking in the ashtray, or otherwise entering the vehicle. If the officer sees a weapon or other evidence of a crime, he will arrest you, search you and the inside of your car, and take you to jail. Obviously, this is not the common result of a traffic stop.

Just because the officer orders you out of the vehicle does not mean that he has decided you are dangerous and that he will give you a hard time. It means only that the officer feels more secure having you out of the car. Once his doubts are dissipated, he is likely to order you back into the car where you are safer from oncoming traffic. Regardless, whether you are inside or outside of your car, it is still only a traffic stop.

Should I try to talk (or cry) my way out of a ticket?

We have all heard of stories of drivers, both male and female, who are able to talk or cry themselves out of a ticket by appealing to the good nature or sympathies of the police officer. They may be just that: stories. If we assume that the police officer is a professional, she will not be swayed by tearful pleas that "my parents will kill me if I get a (or another!) ticket." In fact the professional officer should want parents to know about a young driver's unsafe driving, for it may later save that driver's or another's life.

Never offer money or sexual favors to a police officer in return for not issuing a ticket. This is bribery, which is a crime in every state. By merely offering a bribe, you risk being arrested for and charged with a felony, which carries far more serious consequences than any traffic offense. The motorist who offers a bribe is no better than the rogue police officer who sexually harasses a citizen or offers to overlook a traffic violation in return for sexual favors or money. Motorists offering bribes are likely to be treated harshly by the honest cop, who knows that such motorists encourage the behavior of the unprincipled cop and make it harder for the rest.

Don't act foolishly. Accept the consequences of your traffic violation, or, if you believe that you should not have been ticketed, contest it in court. Don't place yourself in a more dangerous situation which could result in serious legal consequences or loss of your self-respect.

"License and registration, please"

May the officer ask for my driver's license and automobile registration?

Of course. That's how the officer verifies that you are whom you claim to be and that you have a right to be driving the car in which you were stopped. When an officer lawfully stops a vehicle because of a traffic violation, or because of erratic driving which leads the officer to suspect that the motorist is drunk, the officer has the right to see the driver's credentials. Even if you feel you have been stopped illegally, again, the time for challenging this is in court, not by refusing to show your license or registration. While retrieving your registration from the glove compartment, keep in mind that while the compartment door is open, the officer may legally observe its contents from outside of the vehicle.

What if I don't have my license or registration with me?

You have undoubtedly complicated your life, but not greatly. Don't overreact. Not having your driver's license and registration is like not having your credit

card when you want to charge an item in a store or not
having your library card when you want to check a book
out of the library. These are complications, but they are
not the end of the world.

In most locales, if you don't have your license and
registration with you, you'll receive a ticket in addition
to that for the traffic offense which led to the stop. To
satisfy the ticket without paying a fine, you may have to
produce the license at the police station or the court in
a set number of days. In other places, you may have to
pay a fine. These annoyances are obviously minor and,
at most, inconveniences.

These minor repercussions will be the end of it,
but only if you can satisfy the officer, or the officer can
independently verify, that you are whom you claim to
be: a licensed driver with title to or permission to be
driving the car in which you've been stopped. Obviously, if you have other means of identification, you are
likely to satisfy that need. Furthermore, the computerized records of most state motor vehicle record systems
have the physical descriptions that appear on drivers'
licenses. The officer can obtain sufficient information
from that source over his radio to warrant releasing you
with only a ticket. If none of these options is available,
the officer may reasonably detain you for a short period
of time while making other efforts to verify your identity and your right to drive the car. That type of detention is reasonable, as long as you aren't subjected to the
same procedures used for dangerous criminals. The
detention should last no more than a few minutes. Only
in the most extreme situations would it be reasonable
for a police officer to require you to accompany him
anywhere. The ability to verify your identity should be
possible right then and there.

Worse yet, what if I get my license out and find it has expired?

You are not alone. This has happened to the best of us. We tend to forget when our driver's license is due for renewal, until it is time to show it to a police officer. Usually, the result will still be just a traffic ticket. The exact outcome may differ from state to state. Some states may treat this offense more seriously and allow the officer to arrest you, but that outcome is unlikely if the expiration was recent.

You will probably be most concerned about whether the officer will allow you to drive the vehicle home. You may be surprised to learn that most often she will. Alternatively, the officer may require a licensed driver who is along to drive the car, or, at worst, require you to park the car legally, make other arrangements to get home, and have the car picked up later.

You and your car will be separated if the officer takes you into custody. Depending on the written procedures existing in the municipality or state, the officer may have to *impound* your car and have it towed to a storage facility until fines and storage fees are paid. Those procedures may also require that the police make an *inventory* of the vehicle contents. Theoretically, an inventory is meant to protect your property from theft and the police department from false claims of loss. Naturally, an inventory is a search, and any contraband or other criminal evidence which turns up during a lawful inventory may be used as evidence to support a criminal charge against you. I will discuss the problems created by *impoundment* and *inventory* later in this chapter, as well as some alternatives which may exist to limit your exposure and cost.

What if I have never had a valid driver's license or my license was suspended by a traffic or juvenile court judge?

You are in more serious trouble. Here, the procedures vary from state to state. At the very least, the officer will issue a traffic citation ordering you to appear in court. In some states, driving without a valid license or a suspended license is viewed more seriously, and the officer may be required to arrest you. In fact, in some states, conviction of driving with a suspended license carries a mandatory jail sentence of a number of days.

Still other states allow the officer to decide whether to arrest or issue a citation. This decision will be shaped by local department policy and guidelines. Most officers will elect to issue a ticket, unless the driver has a record of repeat offenses. However, there is always a potential problem when police officers are given a choice between issuing a traffic ticket and making an arrest. That discretion may be misused, but unless the abuse is flagrant, there is little recourse. Don't make things worse by attempting to lie your way out of trouble. Because most officers are inclined to issue tickets in this situation, unless required to do otherwise, lying or other hostile behavior from you will only result in an unnecessary trip to the police station.

This time you will not be driving your car home, nor are you likely to be allowed to make alternative arrangements. The car will be impounded, inventoried, and towed, with all of the additional risks and costs associated with having one's car taken.

Moreover, you yourself are not out of the woods. If you are arrested, you will be searched before you are placed in the police car and taken to the police station.

Searching your car

If I am stopped for speeding, and the officer asks if he can search my car, can I say no?

Of course you can say *no*. If the officer has the legal authority to search the car he will not ask in the first place; he will just search the car. *You have a right under the United States Constitution to be free from unreasonable searches and seizures.* A decision to search the car of a speeder or other traffic offender who is being ticketed, but not arrested, is unreasonable unless objective facts and circumstances cause the officer to legitimately believe that he will probably find evidence of a specific crime in the car.

A shaved head and earrings are not the type of facts needed to justify such a legitimate belief. After all, what crime would the officer be alerted to by a shaved head and earrings—counterfeit jewelry? In this free society we do not permit officers to conduct searches based on mere hunches. Nor is a search justified by an officer's subjective feelings, the mere possibility that evidence of a crime is in the car, or the officer's "gut feeling" that a driver is a "druggie." That's why a police officer seeks a driver's consent to search. Consent waives the legal restrictions placed on the police and permits the officer to conduct a search without other legal justification. Consent to a search must be voluntary, which means that it may not be the product of police coercion. But a request from a police officer is not coercion under the law, even though you may feel coerced and not even know that you have the right to refuse. To top it off, the officer needn't tell you that you may refuse.

If you learn nothing more from reading this book, it will have been worthwhile if you come away knowing that you can say no in this situation, even to a uniformed officer.

What happens if the officer conducts an illegal search? Does it make any difference if you call it illegal?

The more cynical reader may suggest that a police officer will search even if the driver says no. That may be true, but it would be an illegal search that violates the Constitution. Evidence found as a result of the illegal warrantless search could not be used by the prosecution to obtain a conviction. While the young speeder in Oklahoma described in Chapter One would still have faced the embarrassment and inconvenience of the arrest and jailing even if he had refused to consent to a search of his car and the officer had searched anyway, the young man would not have faced a criminal conviction in addition to the traffic conviction. Since the prosecution could not use the evidence (the marijuana) obtained from the illegal search, there would be no other evidence to prove the charge of illegal possession of marijuana.

If I don't have marijuana or other illegal items in my car, what do I have to hide? Why shouldn't I consent?

It's a matter of principle and philosophy. The framers of the Bill of Rights thought of the Fourth Amendment as the great right of Americans to be left alone—to do as we please unless our conduct provides sufficient cause to justify police or government interference. This right to privacy is important not only for guilty people; it is vitally important to us all because it draws limits around the power of our government to interfere in our lives and in our comings and goings. It is only if those limits are carefully drawn, respected, and insisted on that they will be there when needed. Besides, if you don't insist on your rights when you have nothing to hide, it is unlikely that you will have the knowledge and *courage* to assert them when you do.

We live in very perilous times when it comes to protecting our privacy. Modern technology has outstripped our ability to preserve our privacy and still live a full life. Moreover, the U.S. Supreme Court has tended, in recent years, to expand government and police power at the expense of individual privacy, allowing the government to use modern technology to accumulate our most personal information. Along the same line, the Court has given police greater authority to detain and search citizens and their automobiles without prior authorization by a judge, as well as allowing courts reviewing searches conducted with warrants to overlook police oversights in the legal process.

While you can do little about the erosion of the Supreme Court's course of action, you don't have to contribute to the erosion of individual liberty by automatically consenting to unnecessary intrusions on your privacy, especially when it is permissible and safe to say no.

Well, if I don't consent, under what circumstances may a police officer search my car anyway?

If you don't consent, the officer must find some justification within the existing legal standards to search the car. If all you have been stopped for is a non-arrestable traffic offense, the car should not be searched. Most simple traffic offenses, such as speeding, illegal turns, and violating traffic signals, are non-arrestable. Consequently, if you are stopped for one of those offenses, there is legal justification for a search only if you consent or if, while talking to you or handing you a ticket, the officer sees a joint or some other illegal object sitting on top of the dashboard or elsewhere in plain view, without the officer's reaching into the car. All it takes is a little common sense to avoid that potential disaster.

While the legal bases for police to conduct warrantless searches of automobiles have increased in the past two decades, there remain limits.

For example, if you are stopped for speeding, and the officer discovers that there is a warrant out for your arrest for failure to appear in court on prior speeding tickets, the officer is required to take you into custody instead of just issuing a traffic ticket. In that case, the officer may search part of your car. The reasons for the search are to protect the officer, by denying you the ability to reach and grab a weapon, and to prevent you from hiding or destroying other evidence. In order to achieve those purposes, the arresting officer may, at the time of your arrest, search only the interior compartment of the vehicle for weapons or evidence. That search extends to compartments, packages, or any other container found in the interior part of the vehicle. The officer may *not*, however, search the trunk of the car.

The officer may search even though you are no longer inside the car or able to reach anything inside the car; you may already be in the back of the police car. Generally, if you are still on the scene and have not yet been transported to the police station, the officer may make the search, supposedly to protect himself and prevent you from destroying evidence.

If you question why it is necessary for the officer's protection (and therefore legal) to search once the driver is out of the car, subdued, and possibly handcuffed and in the police car, you have begun to understand the Supreme Court's attitude toward the police and you. Say the offense for which you have been arrested is driving under suspension, then you may question the other reason offered for allowing this warrantless search—preventing the destruction of evidence. After all, what type of evidence could *exist* relating to driving under suspension? Some state supreme courts share your skepticism and limit the authority of the police in those states to conduct as broad a search as the U.S. Supreme Court allows.

When may an officer search the whole car?

A police officer may search your entire vehicle, including the trunk, when the officer knows of facts that cause her to reasonably believe that evidence of a crime is hidden somewhere in the car. The officer may form this belief based on something you do or say during the stop, something she sees in plain sight inside the car, or some information she gets over the police radio. The fact that cars can be driven away is used to justify this type of search, even though the officer may have the authority to impound the car while seeking a search warrant. Once this authority is activated, the search may extend to every part of the car and everything in it.

While this sounds (and is) terribly broad, there are limits. The officer must have more than a vague, general hunch that young people with unconventional hairstyles or clothing are likely to have drugs on their persons or in their cars. That type of belief does not satisfy the "reasonable belief" requirement. Instead of hunches that give rise to generalities, the officer may act only on specific facts and circumstances that give rise to a belief that a specific crime has been committed and that evidence of that specific crime will be found in the car. Therefore, a police officer's belief that someone driving down the road looks like a criminal, like he is a "druggie," or like he "doesn't belong there," will not suffice. If an officer acts on such unacceptable grounds, the search violates the constitutional prohibition against unreasonable searches and seizures and is illegal. Even if the officer's hunch turns out to be right because she discovers evidence of a crime, the search is still illegal, and the evidence may not be used at a criminal trial.

In order to reach that result, however, the trial court must believe that the officer acted illegally. That is why I have stressed how important it is, whenever you are involved in such an incident, to write down everything you remember about the incident as soon after the event as possible. If anyone is with you when it happens, that person should also provide an independent, detailed written account.

Towing your car

When can my car be towed?

Few aspects of modern life create greater inconvenience than having one's car towed. You may not think it's the most serious event of the day if it accompanies your arrest, but its seriousness will hit you eventually, especially when you retrieve your car. At that time, you'll have to figure out the logistics of getting (without your car) to the place where you must pay your fine and then getting from there (still without your car) to the lot where it's been stored. In large cities, those facilities often aren't close to one another, and you can count on it taking a full, tedious day. You'll probably be stunned when you find out the cost of getting your car back, and then the final hurdle in many communities must be met: a personal check or credit card won't be accepted and you'll have to figure out where to get the cash or a bank check or money order. Running all of these errands wouldn't be half as maddening if you had your car, but obviously that's what this is all about.

A car may be towed by the police, or more often by a private company that has the contract, if it's lawfully impounded. If you're arrested and taken into custody while driving your car, your local community may require the police to *impound* the vehicle. An alternative, of course, would be for the police officer to allow a (sober) licensed driver with you to take custody of the car, or to allow you to park the car legally and return for it when you're released. The police officer *could* allow you to call a relative or friend to come and pick the car up. That is the least likely possibility, however, because you would probably want to wait around until that person arrived, inconveniencing the police officer who would have to wait with you.

Unless your state or local community has provided for these alternatives, the police officer, following your arrest, is permitted to impound the vehicle and have it towed without offering you these less inconvenient options. A car may also be impounded and towed when it is blocking traffic, presenting a hazard to traffic, or illegally parked. Your police department probably has a standardized policy regarding when an officer is required to tow your car and whether, if you are present, she should allow you to make other arrangements. If you are there, request the opportunity to turn it over to a friend or to move it a few feet to a lawful parking spot. The officer may not have to offer you the option unless you initiate the request. Again, knowing you can do something as simple as making a request and taking the initiative may save you a big hassle. Don't be surprised, however, if the options aren't available in your community. Rarely can you avoid a tow by offering to pay the fine and charges when you arrive at the scene of your illegally parked car while it is being connected to a tow truck. Once the switch of the bureaucratic machinery is flipped on, it rarely can be shut off.

If my car is towed, will it be searched?

The standardized procedures which determine when your car is to be towed will also determine whether an inventory of the contents of the car may be made by the police officer or towing authority, and the scope of that inventory. Supposedly, an inventory search is done to protect your property from theft, and the police department from false claims by you that items of value were in the car when it was towed but are not there when the car is returned. For these reasons, inventory searches of impounded vehicles are accepted as legal. Whether the inventory extends to locked compartments, like the glove compartment and trunk, depends on the standardized procedures. Although the need to open every container is questionable, it is permissible if authorized by written policy guidelines which presumably limit the officer's discretion. It hardly serves to limit, however, if the policy authorizes police to open and search every container.

An inventory is not supposed to be a pretext to search for evidence of a crime. However, it may turn out to be just that, and in the end, an inventory of your vehicle is another opportunity for the police to search your car. Anything found during a lawful inventory may provide the basis for criminal charges and may be used to convict you of those charges.

Car towing is so common that it is unwise to transport anything in your car, or to leave anything in your car when it is parked, that you would not want the police or anyone else to discover. Despite claims of limiting police discretion through standardized procedures, the power to impound and then inventory (search) the contents of a car has provided a useful tool to police seeking to conduct a search that cannot be justified in any other way.

Under the influence of drugs or alcohol

When may an officer stop my car because he suspects I am drunk?

Impaired driving resulting from alcohol or drugs is a serious offense. The law treats this matter seriously because drunk drivers are a threat to their own lives and safety, as well as those of anyone else on the road. Consequently, if you are suspected of drunk driving, the police officer who stops you will take it seriously and so should you. If his suspicions are confirmed, you will be arrested and taken to jail, as much for safety as for initiating criminal charges. After all, it would be irrational for a police officer to issue you a ticket and let you drive home if he believes you are drunk. In many states, if you are convicted of drunk driving, the judge will be required to sentence you to jail for three or more days. If you have prior convictions for the same offense, the mandatory time is usually greater.

The law doesn't prohibit drinking and driving; it prohibits *impaired* driving or driving with a certain quantity of alcohol in your system. On the other hand, you don't have to be falling down drunk to be guilty because the law forbids driving under the influence of alcohol. The outcome will turn not only on how much you have had to drink, but also on whether your ability to drive is impaired. *If you are stopped for drunk driving, don't try to talk your way out of it by telling the officer you have only had one or two or a few beers.* First, your partial admission that you have been drinking, but only a little, likely will not be believed, but it is incriminating and will be used against you if the matter comes to trial.Second, a couple or a few beers or glasses of wine *can* impair your driving.

As seriously as society treats this issue, it doesn't permit the police to randomly stop motorists to determine if they have been drinking. Other than at checkpoint stops, a police officer may stop a motorist for drunk driving only if the motorist's conduct leads the officer to reasonably suspect that the driver is impaired. If you seem to be unable to drive within a lane or weave back and forth across lane dividers, you have provided the officer with cause to stop your car to determine if you are drunk. Weaving and crossing the lines is a traffic offense which would allow the officer to stop you and issue a ticket. Even if your weaving isn't bad enough to warrant a ticket, erratic driving allows the officer to order you to stop to find out if you are drunk.

If I am stopped on suspicion of drunk driving, will I automatically be arrested?

If, after the officer talks to you briefly, her suspicions remain, she will order you out of the car and ask you to perform roadside tests of your coordination to help determine your sobriety. Based on several factors, such as your ability to perform these physical tests, whether your speech is coherent or slurred, your appearance and odor, any statements you make, and the officer's observation of your driving, the officer will decide whether you are drunk and should be arrested.

If I am arrested, do I have to take a breath test?

If you are arrested, you may be asked to take a breathalyzer test on the spot, or later at the police station, to determine the alcohol content of your breath. Alternatives to the breathalyzer are blood or urine tests which measure drug and alcohol content.

You have the right to refuse to take these tests, although there are consequences if you do. Your license will probably be revoked because of the refusal, regardless of whether you are convicted of drunk driving. Most states have alternative statutes which punish drunk driving: the first creates a presumption of being under the influence if your breath, alcohol, or urine registers a drug or alcohol content over the legal limit; the second, where no test has been taken, allows a trial court to determine whether a motorist was under the influence based on the arresting officer's testimony about the motorist's appearance and conduct.

If the breath, blood, or urine test is properly administered, guilt is not really contestable. Obviously, it is easier to contest a police officer's conclusions that a motorist was drunk. Consequently, if you have been drinking, it is rarely advisable to consent to taking the test, realizing of course that the refusal will probably result in suspension of your license. But if you are convicted, your license will be suspended as well. Many communities now use video cameras to record the conduct, appearance, and speech of those charged with drunk driving, finding often that, even without the test, conviction is unavoidable when the video is shown in court.

You would be surprised how often a person who honestly convinces himself that he wasn't drunk is forced to confront a different reality after viewing himself on tape. Let's face it, if your driving is impaired, your ability to measure the level of your impairment may also be affected. The best way to protect yourself from the legal consequences of drunken driving is not to drink or use drugs *and* drive.

Can I ask to consult an attorney before consenting to take a sobriety test?

If you have been doing some light drinking, and you were initially stopped for an unrelated reason, such as speeding or an equipment violation, it may be a close call as to whether you will "pass" the breath test and avoid conviction. In this case, your decision on whether to take the test will be a difficult one, and you may want to call an attorney for advice. If so, ask the officer for access to a phone and a chance to talk in private. This request should be honored, but not always before your decision on whether to take the test has to be made. This is because most states have regulations requiring the test to be given within a certain time of your driving to be valid, and thus, if this period is close to expiring, the officer may demand that you make your decision before taking the time to consult a lawyer.

Sobriety checkpoints

I went through a drunk driving checkpoint and was very nervous. I thought you said I could not be stopped without cause.

I did say that, but . . . . Society's extreme concern for impaired driving has led to the creation of roadblocks, where every motorist traveling on the highway must stop momentarily, or at least slow to a crawl, and be checked briefly and superficially for signs of drinking. Not too many years ago, the Fourth Amendment to the U.S. Constitution would have forbidden such a stop without a law enforcement official's having a specific reason to believe that the driver was impaired. Society's growing concern with and attention to the problem of drunk driving coincided with the Supreme Court's increased tendency to limit the Fourth Amendment right to be left alone, factors which led to the approval of these checkpoint stops.

If you come to a sobriety checkpoint, expect to be stopped and very briefly examined for signs of intoxication. Don't attempt to drive through it without stopping because you will endanger yourself and others. You will also be arrested.

You may be required to come to a full stop or just slow down to a crawl. An officer will ask you to roll down your window to find out whether you show visible signs of drinking or whether your speech is slurred. To test for the presence of alcohol, the officer may shine a light in your eyes to measure their reaction. There is even a device capable of measuring the air quality within a few inches of the driver. Most often, the delay encountered by waiting in line and the brief encounter with the officer is the full extent of the intrusion and you will be sent on your way. There can be no further intrusion unless, during this brief encounter, the officer detects signs that you are, indeed, under the influence.

What happens if I do show signs of drinking at the checkpoint?

If those signs exist, you can expect further sobriety tests. You'll be requested to drive out of the line over to an area where you may be asked additional questions. As an officer's suspicion that you are drunk escalates, the intrusion will escalate. You'll be asked to get out of the car to determine whether you can move without showing signs of impairment; failure here will lead to full roadside sobriety tests. In other words, initially the officer can do little but observe your speech and general coherence. If the signs of impairment appear, the officer can do more. Ultimately, if you fail the roadside coordination tests, you will be arrested.

Keep in mind, a police officer may not pull you over, other than at a checkpoint, unless you have provided the officer with cause by committing a traffic offense or by erratic driving which would lead to a reasonable suspicion that you are drunk or drug-impaired. Checkpoints are the only permissible way to stop all motorists, including those who have given no reason to believe they may be drunk.

If I see a checkpoint ahead, can I avoid it?

Sobriety checkpoints are relatively new. Thus, it isn't clear what you can do to avoid one once you see it ahead on the road. In fact, their effectiveness is questionable. At times, as cars wait in line to move up to the checkpoint, drivers and passengers change places. I have even heard of drivers paying money to passengers in other cars to switch and drive the car through the checkpoint. Obviously, this can only happen where there is back-up and delay and drivers who wish to court disaster by making poor decisions.

There is legal support for the position that you may turn around or off the road to avoid the checkpoint, if you do so in a non-reckless manner, without the police being allowed to pursue and stop you. And, if you have been drinking, you won't be any worse off even if you avoid the checkpoint, are stopped, and the stop is later upheld in court, than if you go through the checkpoint, provided your avoidance is done safely. Moreover, some states require publicity beforehand and publication of the location of a checkpoint so that motorists can avoid them. It is likely, however, now that the Supreme Court has sanctioned the use of checkpoints without such requirements, that publicity requirements and options to avoid stopping may disappear. A court in Indiana even upheld the stop of a motorist who made a lawful U-turn to avoid a sobriety checkpoint, claiming that the evasive action was a fair indication that the motorist was drunk.

I was stopped at a license checkpoint and my license and car were checked. Is this legal?

This type of check predates sobriety checkpoints. In order to assure that only licensed drivers are driving or that automobiles meet minimum safety requirements, roadblocks may be set up compelling all drivers to produce a valid driver's license and have their cars minimally tested for safety, such as an inspection for operational brake lights.

Other than at a roadblock, a police officer may not choose which drivers and which cars to stop and test. The roadblocks are allowed, instead, so that police do not have the discretion to discriminate based on their personal prejudices. Other than at a roadblock, a police officer may not stop a car to check for safety, unless real facts exist to alert the officer to an unsafe condition.

Accidents

I am more concerned about accidents. What should I do if I am involved in one?

Sooner or later, almost everyone is involved in an automobile accident. How's that for being grim? Hopefully, both you and the other driver are insured, as more and more states now require insurance or proof of financial responsibility following an accident. *Be sure to have insurance information in your car whenever you drive: the name of the insurance company, its claims office telephone number, and your policy number.*

If you are involved in an accident, local law and your insurance policy dictate what you must do, but step one everywhere is to check whether there are any injuries and, if there are, to render assistance. But, be careful when rendering assistance, for you would be surprised how many lawsuits are fought over whether a would-be helper worsened the injuries of the person who was "helped." Most of us are not medical professionals and can't know if we are helping or making injuries worse. Ordinarily, if someone cannot move on his or her own, you should not move that person. Instead, you should summon assistance. But use your common sense. If a car is on fire and an entrapped person cannot move, that person has to be helped out one way or another because the fire threatens greater disaster than almost any harm you could cause.

Let's presume that no one is hurt and you must deal with less serious and threatening matters. Many states and communities require you to summon a police officer to the scene of an accident, even if no one is hurt. In the busiest of cities, you may be told that no officer will be sent to the scene, but that you should go to the police station within a day and file an accident report. If, on the other hand, you are waiting for a police officer, focus foremost on your safety and that of the other driver. Predictably, both of you will be rattled and could get in the way of oncoming traffic.

Don't admit fault because your insurance policy probably prohibits you from doing so. Exchange information. Show each other your driver's licenses and the card from your insurance company.

Avoid an argument with the other driver. Regardless of whose fault the accident is, it can't be undone. Nor can you settle liability by arguing it out with the driver. In any event, that's why you both (hopefully) have insurance. There is nothing wrong with apologizing to the other driver if you are at fault, but make your apology general.

If you're in a community where the police don't need to be summoned, be sure you see the other driver's license and/or other documentation to make sure he or she doesn't give you a false identity. That is more common than you might expect. If a police officer arrives on the scene, you will give all of that information to the officer, who will include it in the accident report. The officer will try to ascertain fault and may issue a traffic ticket. If the cars can be driven, you'll then be allowed to leave. If your car can't be driven, the police officer will assist you in having it towed and will help you get home or to transportation.

Be sure to notify your insurance company within the next twenty-four hours. If you were issued a ticket as a result of the accident, tell the insurance company that, too.

What if I was driving someone else's car when I had the accident, or (groan) someone else was driving my car?

It is difficult to generalize about insurance coverage. Ordinarily, your insurance coverage works both ways. If you have lent your car to another licensed driver, your car insurance will cover the car, unless this violates the terms of your policy. Similarly, if you are driving someone else's car, the car owner's insurance should cover you, but your own insurance should cover you as well.

Obviously, the best thing to do is check the policy first or call the company's toll-free number for information. If you do make the phone call, record the name of the person who supplies the information in case the company later claims it is incorrect.

Your particular policy may contain specific limitations, and the outcome will be determined by the specific provisions of the policy. That is more likely to be true if the person driving your car is under age twenty-one or twenty-five. Some policies exclude coverage for drivers not specifically named who are under a set age.

3 WHEN TRAVELING

Americans travel a great deal, and only a tiny percentage of that travel relates to transportation of illegal drugs or other illegal activity. However, that illegal activity, naturally, attracts the attention of law enforcement. Second, then, to cars, in terms of being the focus of significant police attention, are travel by plane, by bus, and, to a lesser extent, by train. Our law has been shaped and bent to allow police maximum latitude in seeking out and prosecuting the tiny percentage of criminal elements. However, that latitude affects us all. When traveling through an airport or bus station, it is important to understand your rights and the powers of investigating police officers.

Passengers at airports and bus terminals are not treated at all alike by the police. Police conduct is bold when dealing with bus passengers. The Immigration and Naturalization agent referred to in Chapter One did not follow me onto the bus. Today, he might. It isn't at all surprising that police aggressively intercept passengers in bus terminals and, now, even those already on buses. Passengers are apt to be younger and poorer than other travelers, people with the least amount of political and economic power and, therefore, less likely than other groups to successfully challenge these police practices. You won't find police officers boarding airplanes and harassing passengers. Could you imagine the outcry from business executives if police started "working" the planes? Nonetheless, if intercepted at an airport, it is helpful to know where your rights begin and official authority ends.

Airport security checkpoints

I know what an airport magnetometer is supposedly testing for, but I've often wondered if there are other reasons for looking through my hand-carried luggage. Are there?

A magnetometer located at the entrance to a con-course, or departure gate, is there to test for weapons. The practice was initiated at a time when airplane hijacking was becoming uncomfortably common. Mag-netometers are used in other contexts now, such as at the entrance to some public buildings and courthouses. The device x-rays hand-carried luggage and other pack-ages that a traveler intends to carry onto the airplane. At the same time, the traveler walks through a device which emits a sound if the person is carrying a metallic object which could be a weapon. If the x-ray focuses on an object that could be a weapon or the person walking through the device sets it off, the traveler will not be allowed to proceed until he satisfies the attendant that the object is not a weapon. Similarly, video cameras will be inspected and opened to make sure that they do not contain a bomb or other explosive. In fact, these tests are of limited effectiveness. They track and locate conventional weapons. As we learned in the Pan Am/ Lockerbie, Scotland tragedy, these devices do not detect plastic explosives and similar high-tech devices used by terrorists.

The magnetometer and accompanying devices are limited searches and involve intrusions on our right of privacy. We accept, and may even welcome, them because we have become accustomed to them, and because of the safety that their use promises. In other words, most of us are willing to surrender some privacy in return for security. In the end, of course, we have to decide how much privacy we are willing to surrender in return for additional security. The magnetometer works indiscriminately. All passengers are subjected to it, not just those picked out by law enforcement officers or airline attendants. We know in advance that, in order to gain access to the concourse, we will have to pass through the magnetometer, and we elect to do so. It is not at all like a search where an individual is unexpectedly singled out. Moreover, the intensity of the magnetometer search is very unintrusive. The important thing to understand is that these searches are limited searches for weapons designed to prevent hijacking, and not broader searches for evidence of other crimes.

If I activate an airport magnetometer can I avoid further investigation by choosing not to pass beyond the security checkpoint into the boarding area?

There is no definitive answer. Some courts have held that even after activating a magnetometer, a prospective passenger may refuse to submit to a search for weapons and instead forfeit her ability to travel by air. This result serves the purpose of the whole procedure, which is not to catch criminals, but rather to keep armed hijackers from getting on airplanes.

Not surprisingly, this is not a universally accepted viewpoint. Wouldn't you be suspicious of the person who, after activating the magnetometer, suddenly remembers that she is carrying something which she wishes to keep private? Just as you are likely to be suspicious, some courts have allowed airport personnel to search passengers who just walk away from the security checkpoint, rather than allowing them to walk away and surrender their right to travel by air. These courts are concerned that if, in fact, the traveler is carrying a weapon, there is no guarantee that the traveler will not return later when the checkpoint is busier and manage to evade the screening devices. However, it is important to remember that all courts limit these

searches to searches for weapons, and the searches are
not to be expanded into general ones for contraband.

Airport luggage searches

**I'm a student, and when I got off of a plane from Florida after
Spring break, I was surrounded by "feds" who treated me like
Public Enemy Number 1. Why feds, and why me?**

At airports around the country today, several law
enforcement agencies share authority. Overall authority
rests with the local police, but several federal agencies
have jurisdictional authority that carries into local airports. Some of these agencies are concerned with insur-
ing airport safety and others are involved in trying to
apprehend drug couriers. If the people who stopped you
identified themselves as federal officers, they were
probably from the Drug Enforcement Administration.

The more interesting question is "Why me?" Federal and local law enforcement agencies try to make it
seem as though they have perfected a science when
talking about which travelers at airports they choose to
intercept and question about drugs. I think, rather than
a science, the answer to your question is similar to the
one Sir Edmund Hillary gave when asked why he
climbed Mount Everest, "because it was there." That is
probably about as scientific as the officers' decision to
stop you.

The more technical answer is that officers operating at airport concourses work from a "drug courier
profile," which theoretically captures the characteristics of travelers who are transporting drugs. The profile
is "confidential," so as not to tip off the prey, but many
of the characteristics are based on common sense or
have been disclosed in court cases. Some of the characteristics make sense and might be considered reasonably reliable justifications for investigation. For example, airline ticket agents working at airports are
encouraged to notify law enforcement officers when

someone appears shortly before a plane's departure and pays cash for a ticket to a destination city from which the person plans to return immediately. Of course, the person could be dropping off something other than contraband, but the mode of travel and the use of cash certainly raises suspicions which would warrant inquiry. Most people, however, who are stopped in airport concourses do not give such obvious signals.

We are told that a traveler may be dogged by drug agents if he leaves the plane last (or first), looks around nervously, has no luggage except that which he carries on board, and leaves the airport terminal rapidly. These characteristics describe me and most people I know. It describes the nervous flier, the traveler in a hurry who doesn't want to wait for luggage, and the traveler who doesn't trust the airlines to deliver checked luggage on time and in reasonably good condition. Obviously, these characteristics are broad and meaningless enough to cover virtually every traveler except the grandmother over seventy with teased, blue hair. In fact, that is such a great cover for a drug courier, I now expect the profile to be expanded to cover people with teased, blue hair.

I can probably guess the characteristics that caused the police to single you out and not others. You probably looked and dressed like a student, and coming from Florida didn't help since it's considered a drug distribution center. Of course, during Spring break, hundreds of thousands of young people fit that description, but the unlikelihood of picking a needle from a haystack does not deter these drug fighters.

They grabbed me aside, checked my ticket and driver's license, and then fortunately let me go after I let them look through my luggage. Did they have the authority to do this?

You haven't been following me. If your description of your encounter with the federal agents is accurate, you were illegally seized and held, while they checked your credentials and searched your suitcase, all in violation of your Fourth Amendment rights.

I'm sure that, if I spoke with these federal agents, they would tell me, as they would have told a court if the search of your suitcase had led to the discovery of drugs, that your description of what happened is totally inaccurate. Rather than grabbing you as you say, these agents would claim that they politely intercepted you on your way through the concourse, identified themselves, and then politely asked if you would step aside to talk with them.

Quite different, isn't it, from your recollection of the events? They had no legal authority to grab you or block your way. Dressing like a student and coming from Florida didn't give the police legal justification to delay you, any more than they can stop you in an automobile just because you're a student. As simply put as possible, in a free society, people must be free to come and go as they please unless *their* conduct, coupled with external conditions, provide sufficient cause to interfere with that right. Just as in your car, a law enforcement officer may not compel you to stop on foot unless the officer has a reasonable, factual basis to believe you are involved in criminal activity. Even if the officer has the basis to stop you, this is not reason enough to search your luggage. Like the car search, the officer must either formally and legally arrest you or have reasonable cause to believe your luggage probably contains evidence of a specific crime in order to seize it.

Since your dress and state of departure certainly did not provide sufficient cause, any encounter between you and the agents was either consensual on your part or illegal on their part. Touching you or otherwise indicating—through their tone of voice, the words used, or conduct which might have blocked your way—that you were not free to disregard their requests led you to conclude that you lacked the freedom to simply go on your way. Any reasonable person would have drawn the same conclusion, thus making this an illegal curtailment of your freedom, since there was not sufficient cause to support it. As an example, if the agents held on to your driver's license and ticket when they asked to search your belongings, that would be evidence that you were not free to leave and the federal agents thus conducted an illegal investigative stop.

In an encounter which rests, for its legal justification, on the consent of the individual, that person must feel free to ignore the requests to stop, to chat, and to step aside, in favor of simply walking away. After all, that is the significance of consent. I would go so far as to suggest that, even if the encounter took place exactly as the agents might suggest it did, reasonable Americans would not feel free to disregard law enforcement officers' requests nor to refuse to stop and talk with them, unless told by the agents that it is permissible to do so.

Law enforcement officers in airport terminals capitalize on this ignorance. They pay no attention to a traveler's attempts to avoid talking with them, following the traveler through the concourse, seeking to change the traveler's mind before she leaves the terminal. Their conduct is calculated to create the impression that the person should stop and cannot simply ignore their requests.

What exactly is the significance of the stop being illegal?

First, it signifies that the method of doing business adopted by agencies of our government is calculated to violate constitutional rights. Second, and of primary importance to the person stopped, any information gained or evidence discovered by the agents as a result of their illegal conduct may not be used to prove criminal charges resulting from the encounter. Because most people stopped are not, in fact, carrying contraband, the remedy applies to very few, and even these few must persuade a court that their version of the facts surrounding the encounter is the truth, rather than a cleaned-up version presented by the government.

This type of illegal conduct has intangible effects on all of us, the vast majority of whom are not carrying contraband or doing anything else illegal. It is unsettling to be the subject of a police inquiry, especially when you don't fully understand what is going on, why you have been targeted, and what your rights are under the circumstances. Many people will undoubtedly feel conflict in such a situation, feeling that what's going on isn't right, but fearful about antagonizing the investigators. Most of us would be rattled by having someone rummaging through our belongings, and some people will be carrying perfectly legal objects which they would prefer not to have others know about. If nothing else, the inquiry will delay the traveler for at least a few minutes. However, the disturbing effect will likely last longer.

Even for those of us who pose no interest to these police and federal agents, most of us will have children or grandchildren who do. It is troubling to think that they may be picked out of a crowd on nothing but a hunch and subjected to these inquiries.

Stopped by airport security

Remember, I'm not a lawyer. I'm not looking for a hassle. How should I respond when stopped by a police officer or DEA agent in an airport?

If you follow my directions you will minimize the chances of a hassle and, hopefully, eliminate the possibilities for later legal troubles. The importance of clarifying the situation at the outset can't be overstated. It will give you a moment to calm yourself and remember how to proceed. It will also force the police or federal agents to clarify whether they are *ordering* you to stop or merely *asking* you to stop and cooperate.

One way to determine this is to completely ignore the officer, say "no," and keep walking. However, that's not necessarily the best way to handle the situation. As I said earlier, if the officer isn't prepared to force you to comply, he may ignore your refusal and walk along next to you, repeating his request and forcing you to steadfastly maintain your refusal. On the other hand, if the officer is prepared to force you to comply, he won't allow you to walk away, and you will have certainly clarified the situation. If the officer forces you to comply and orders you to stop by placing a hand on you or blocking your path, call it to his attention and inform him that you are not stopping willingly. If this happens, by no means change the nature of the encounter by consenting to a search. *Certainly don't physically resist, but don't consent.*

I don't think I can handle just ignoring the officer. Is there another course of action I can take to determine the officer's intentions?

This isn't the only way to handle the situation, and I'm not sure that it's the best way for everyone. There is a middle road, though.

If you're stopped while walking through an airport terminal, or a train or bus terminal for that matter, by a person who identifies herself as a law enforcement officer, make sure that you check the individual's identification. Don't just accept a wallet flipped open and quickly flipped closed before you have a chance to read it. You want to make sure that the person is in fact whom she claims to be. The agency which the officer represents will be clearly indicated on the identification, which will help you to know why you're being stopped. Equally important, you have helped to set the tone for this encounter. These investigators are not used to people turning the tables and insisting that they identify themselves. Remember, all of this is taking place in a very public setting. The agent's reactions will be tempered by that fact and likely she will want to appear cooperative and nonthreatening, at least to people passing by.

After checking her identification, it is time to ascertain the officer's intentions. Ask her if you are required to stop. She will probably try to divert your attention by asking you questions. Insist on knowing whether she is demanding that you stop. If it's the usual dragnet sweep of a terminal, she won't have legal justification to require you to stop, but she doesn't want to tell you that. Let her know politely that you won't cooperate unless you know whether your cooperation is being requested or required. If she won't tell you, then I would advise you to start walking towards the gate or the exit and force her hand. The officer will probably, though reluctantly, indicate that she is only *asking* for your cooperation. Make sure that she uses words which express what she means. Insist on clarification until you understand what is happening.

Once you find out that she is requesting your assistance, it's completely up to you whether to comply. It's easiest if you decide at the outset either to comply with all requests, including a request to open your suitcases or other packages, or comply with no requests for information or to search. It is terribly foolish to think that you can play a cat-and-mouse game with the inquiring officer. You will lose that one if you try. At some point, the information that you willingly offer may provide sufficient legal justification for the officer to force you to cooperate. That justification, however, never extends to requiring you to open your suitcase unless she is arresting you (and even then it is not altogether certain) or if she believes you are carrying a bomb or other dangerous device.

After the encounter, as always, be sure to write down what happened, making careful note of what the officer said which led you to believe that she was *ordering* or *asking* you to do something.

What I've prescribed here isn't as difficult as you may think. You're not defying authority; you're merely finding out whether or not you have a choice in the matter. This conversation will probably be relatively civil in a very public setting, both of which should reduce your anxiety. By asking these questions, you're not being overly aggressive, but correctly assertive. You can do it. Take heart; the police actions in airports are far less coercive than what is taking place on buses.

Using someone else's airline ticket

Will I have problems if I use discounted tickets to travel?

Not a few people today travel on discounted tickets purchased on a secondary market from an original purchaser who ultimately finds that he cannot use the ticket. Naturally, in a market where many airline tickets are not refundable, the airline wants to honor the ticket only if it is used under the terms of the purchase. Many airlines will refuse, in fact, to honor a ticket if the traveler is not the person whose name appears on the ticket. They don't ordinarily check tickets against drivers' licenses or other identification because that would cause delay and irritate the airline's customers. But if the information is available, the airline employees checking in passengers are instructed not to honor the ticket.

Since there appears to be a cooperative working arrangement between the airlines and government agents, whereby the latter are notified by ticket agents of passengers who use cash (especially from large rolls) to purchase tickets, it is not unlikely that the arrangement works two ways. When investigating agents encounter a passenger whose identification does not match the name on the ticket, those agents may be providing the information to the airlines, which will use the information and possibly refuse to honor the ticket and permit the traveler to fly. This arrangement is not apt to be acknowledged, but the airlines are especially keen on halting the traffic in airline tickets.

Can the airline really refuse to honor a ticket if it is in a different name than that of the person presenting it? And can they seize the ticket?

The airlines enter into a contract with you when you purchase a ticket. You promise to use the ticket under the conditions attached at the time of sale, and the airlines promise to fly you to your destination, hopefully safely and on time. One of the conditions attached at the time of sale is that the ticket can't be transferred from you to anyone else. If the ticket isn't refundable, you're out of luck. Obviously, there is an active secondary market for airline tickets (read the ads in any major newspaper). These sales are, however, contrary to the conditions under which the tickets were issued, and the airline won't honor the ticket if it knows that the prospective passenger is not the same person whose name appears on the ticket.

The U.S. Department of Transportation and the Federal Aviation Agency back up the airlines completely on this point. The airlines claim that there is a constant market for stolen tickets, and the nontransferability policy helps to combat ticket thefts. Whether that is true or not, the government has not contested the policy. The airlines also claim that nontransferability is required by FAA regulations that require the airlines to maintain a manifest with the names of passengers on every flight that departs from every airport. However, these regulations don't require the airlines to refuse to honor transferred tickets; they merely require them to accurately record the names of departing passengers. Obviously, if the airlines dropped their policy regarding nontransferability, passengers would indicate their correct identities at check-in, which would satisfy federal regulations.

Traveling by bus

I don't own a reliable car and can't afford to fly. Travel by bus is the only way I can go, but you've scared me. Should I stay away from buses?

It isn't necessary for you to stay off buses or away from bus terminals. However, it's necessary that you know your rights and how to assert them.

I've heard that police are "working the buses." What does this mean?

"Working the buses" is a phenomenon of the 1990's related to the police effort to combat drug trafficking. The police can't tell who the drug dealers are, so they hassle everyone on a bus trying to determine whether anyone is carrying drugs. In the process, they disturb everyone's privacy.

When police officers work a bus, they board just a few minutes before it's time for the bus to depart. Timing is part of the psychological assault. When dealing with the officers, a passenger is concerned about being taken off the bus and missing its departure. A passenger may also be worried about causing a delay in the bus's departure and angering fellow passengers with whom he'll be traveling for several hours or more. The police use these natural concerns to increase the pressure on bus passengers not to resist police requests for information and permission to search suitcases and other possessions.

Once one or two officers board a bus and stand near the entrance, the aisle and exit are effectively blocked. The officers proceed up the aisle checking out each passenger, engaging the passengers in conversation and requesting permission from each to open suitcases and other packages.

May I leave if I don't want to open my suitcase or am afraid of dealing with these officers?

You have every right to get out of your seat, gather your possessions, and leave the bus. However, it will take some courage to ask the police officers to get out of your way and to let you pass by them. You understand, of course, that they'll be suspicious of your decision to suddenly change your travel plans and will credit that decision to their unexpected presence on the bus. Nonetheless, they must let you pass and leave the bus if that is your decision. They may hassle you about the decision, but, if you remain firm, they have no legal authority to detain you. Understand the difficulty, however, in trying to ease by one or two police officers standing in the small aisle of an interstate bus. Unless they move and make room, it is virtually impossible to get by. The psychological effect on you caused by their blocking the aisle is clearly intentional.

But why leave? You have the right to remain on the bus unmolested by the police, as well as by other passengers. You don't have to leave the bus to avoid questioning or having the police go through your belongings.

But if I remain, do I have to do what they tell me to do?

Absolutely not. Keep in mind that you have the power to control what happens. It may take more courage than it should to exercise that power, but it is yours to exercise. Don't wait for the police to inform you that you have the power; they won't.

Police officers have the same right as anyone else to walk up to a stranger and start asking questions. Of course, if a stranger walked up to you and started asking direct questions, you would immediately walk away or look around for a police officer to call for assistance. We tend to treat police officers differently than we treat others. Rather than walk away, we tend to provide the information and to cooperate because we assume that police wouldn't ask if they didn't have the power to demand our compliance. The point is, they have the power *to ask but not to force* you to comply with their requests. They are counting on you to misunderstand this and believe that you must do what they ask.

Instead of having to comply, *you have the right to terminate the conversation.* While the police may persist, annoyingly asking why you—unlike your fellow passengers—refuse to cooperate, you are completely within your rights in refusing. You would be amazed at how this exchange would be portrayed in court, allowing a judge to find that any conversation or cooperation was consensual on your part, and not the result of police coercion. You wouldn't recognize the conversation, or if you recognize the words, you wouldn't the tone. So persist in your refusal, knowing that you are acting in the tradition of the great right of Americans to be left alone, unless a police officer has justifiable cause to interfere with that right.

If I refuse to cooperate, will that give the officer justifiable cause to order me off the bus?

No. Forcing you off the bus for doing nothing except exercising your constitutional right to privacy would be a false arrest. More importantly, the officer knows it would be a false arrest, exposing him to liability for damages. You don't need to tell him the law, nor is it advisable. The officer childishly may take that as a dare and seek to teach you a lesson. Instead, it's important that you know the law and know the limits of the officer's authority, so that you may assert your rights successfully.

Since forcing you off the bus and causing you to miss the bus's departure is an arrest, this is lawful only when the officer has reasonable cause to believe that you're committing a crime. Reasonable cause, under these circumstances, wouldn't result from your refusal to cooperate. It would only arise if the officer discovers contraband in your belongings, and that contraband could be used as evidence to convict only if it were found as a result of a search based on a valid consent or justifiable cause provided by your conduct or statements. Alternatively, reasonable cause could arise if the police had reliable information that a specific passenger is carrying contraband; the officers could arrest that person after determining which passenger reasonably fits the description.

If you believe that an officer has no legal right to force you off the bus or arrest you, don't physically resist, but take careful mental notes on what is happening so that you can fight the officer's conduct later—in court.

I'm not willing to tell a police officer to buzz off, but I draw the line at having him look through my suitcase. Can I be friendly and tell the officer where I'm headed and why, but then say no when he asks to look in my suitcase?

Just as long as your conversation with the police officers doesn't provide them with justifiable cause to believe that you're committing a crime, you're still in control. The officer's continued authority to act still depends on your consent. Simply telling the police your destination doesn't provide them with cause to make an arrest or search your luggage. I would suggest, though, that as a result of your abrupt reversal from cooperation to adamant refusal, you'll be subjected to at least several repeated requests by the police to let them look into your suitcase. Face it, your curiosity would be aroused in similar circumstances. However, curiosity over a person's exercising of his rights doesn't allow the police to arrest you or force you to let them look into your possessions.

Ideally, you should say "no" at the outset and not provide the officers with any information or reason to think that, because of your change of mind, you have something to hide. Nonetheless, *you have an absolute right to withhold your consent* to a luggage search.

Don't relent, and save yourself the trouble of telling them that you have this "thing" about people going through your clothes. One excuse only makes another necessary when the excuse doesn't satisfy the other person. Even if your reason is true, it's not likely to satisfy the officers. They may even promise not to touch your things if you'll move everything around at their direction. Now what do you do? You either relent and let them search or finally reach the bottom line and "Just Say No"! Why try to make excuses when you don't have to explain your refusal? Sooner or later, you always have to get to that bottom line.

How long may officers delay the bus's departure?

As we all know, public transportation schedules are not cast in stone. Nonetheless, police may not unreasonably delay the departure because such delay may cast doubt on the voluntariness of the passengers' willingness to cooperate. If police give the impression that the bus won't be permitted to leave until all of the passengers comply with the officers' request for information and permission to search, subsequent compliance could hardly be termed voluntary. Instead, it would be a submission to an illegal show of authority.

4 IN YOUR HOME

Ah, home alone. What you do at home is your business. It's the one place where you can relax, where you don't have to keep up your guard. Everyone needs a place where you don't have to explain your dress, speech, habits, or associates. Don't misunderstand. That doesn't mean that you aren't required to abide by the law in your home. But as long as your conduct isn't particularly obvious, doesn't result in harm to any person, and doesn't disturb those around you, home is generally where your conduct will go unnoticed.

Provided you take minimal precautions, your personal peace of mind while at home should be assured. If you had to take extraordinary precautions it would mean that even at home your personal security is provisional. What do I mean by minimal precautions? Simple: If you don't want the world to know the contents of your conversations, don't engage in shouting matches, oblivious to the proximity of your neighbors. If you don't want the world to know what you're doing, don't do it while parading in front of the windows at night with the lights on and the shades up. In other words, common sense should be sufficient to protect ordinary privacy.

Unfortunately, even common sense doesn't always work. American legal principles, and their English forebears, have always subscribed to the notion that "a man's home is his castle." However, that castle is not as impenetrable as it once was. Courts are now more willing to allow the government to use modern technology to gather masses of information about us without ever having to get prior permission from a judge, or ever having to justify why it wanted that information.

Is Big Brother really watching?

Okay, I'm curious. What kind of information?

There is little the police or other governmental agencies can't find out about you these days. Nineteen eighty-four came and went, and Big Brother is still watching.

For starters, the police can hire an airplane and fly over your backyard filming you sunbathing and whatever else is visible from above. A mail cover allows the post office, at the request of another government or police agency, to keep track of people sending you mail and organizations sending you literature through the mail. A pen register at the phone company may be installed at police request to collect the numbers dialed to and from your home telephone. Police or other governmental agencies may have access to your cancelled checks and deposit records to find out who is writing checks to you and to whom you are writing checks. Library and film rental records disclose what you are reading and what you are watching. Even the trash you discard may be examined to see what you are throwing away.

No doubt by now you've realized that the accumulation of this information provides a fairly complete and accurate picture about a person, including her health, friends, lovers, political and religious activities, and even beliefs. Figure that, if the Gillette razor company knows when it's your eighteenth birthday to send you a sample razor, your government, with its super, interconnecting computers, knows much more about you.

Give me a break. Why would anyone want that information about me?

That's just the point. The information may be gathered without anyone ever having to explain why. It's possible that your earlier conduct justifies the police in wanting this information, but then again maybe you merely angered someone in a position of authority. The problem is that the information may be accumulated regardless of whether it is for a good, bad, or nonexistent reason, without any official ever having to explain why.

The police are at the door

All right, all right. If they want to go to all that trouble to find out about me, let them. I'm more concerned about the police officer who comes to my door.

Then I have some good news for you. The authority of a police officer to get past your front door is highly regulated. *Essentially, there are three ways for the officer to get into your apartment or house. If you choose to let him in, then he's there by your consent. Otherwise, a police officer can enter your home only after she's obtained prior judicial approval to enter (a warrant), or when a near emergency situation exists that allows her to enter without a warrant.*

When must I consent to the officer entering my home?

The whole idea of consent is that it is completely your choice whether to consent to a police officer's entry. Consent must be voluntary, which in this case means free from official coercion. The officer can't say or do anything which would lead you to believe that you aren't free to refuse her entry. However, even an unwise decision may be consensual. When evidence is discovered as a result of a consensual search, the fact that the individual acted unwisely against his best interests doesn't negate the consent or raise questions about its voluntariness. Obviously, the officer wants in. She isn't obligated to tell you that you have the right to refuse her request. In a limited manner, she can even repeat and persist in her requests for entry.

Don't debate the issue with the police officer. This may be interpreted as evidence that you were in complete control, rather than that you were quaking in your boots, trying to work up the courage to say "no." Moreover, don't feel the necessity to tell the police officer the law—that she needs a warrant to get in. Presume that she knows about warrants. Be prepared to feel somewhat confused when she responds that she doesn't need a warrant and again asks to come into your house. She's right. Of course she doesn't need a warrant—*if you consent*. Once you refuse, the officer's only legal recourse is to try and get a warrant to gain entry.

Make your decision and then act on it. Don't expect the officer to like you when you say "no," but she isn't at your door in search of a new friend. If the officer wants to enter your house because she believes a crime is being committed or because she's looking for evidence of a crime, your interests and hers aren't the same. Once you make the decision to refuse her entry, in the words of a former First Lady: Just Say No!

Be mindful that you may place conditions on your consent, so that the officer's entry is dependent on the specific terms of your consent, i.e., whether she can do any actual searching or just look around or which rooms she can enter. However, set those terms at the outset. Don't try to outsmart her thinking you can alter the terms if she gets too close for comfort. In the best of situations, someone else will be present who later can attest to your claims about the limited nature of the consent.

Consent to search given by another

Can my landlord allow a police officer to search my apartment?

Your landlord has the right to enter your apartment to make necessary repairs. Unless the lease you signed allows the landlord to come into your apartment as he or she sees fit, access to your apartment for purposes other than to check a dangerous condition or to make repairs isn't part of a standard landlord-tenant agreement. A lease is a contract. In return for your promise to pay rent and meet other specified conditions, the owner promises to let you occupy the premises without interfering with or disturbing your privacy. Allowing someone in to search your apartment would be a gross interference with that privacy.

These basic rules, however, may not apply in every situation. You may not live in a large apartment house with an impersonal management. Many young people rent apartments, rooms, or even hovels carved out of large houses, with the owner living in adjacent quarters. Here the same general rules apply. Even though the owner has a key, it would be unreasonable for police to assume that the owner has the authority to let them into your apartment. Even if you merely rent a room in a house, your privacy should be similarly guarded, although a court might be less inclined to restrict the owner's access and authority to admit others if the room is accessible to the owner at all times.

While the same rules that apply to large apartment houses apply to alternative rental arrangements as well, they don't always work as effectively. Your privacy depends on your landlord's willingness to respect it. I remember living in an apartment in a large old house in a college town, when my wife, who had arrived home from work earlier than usual and was sitting in the living room reading our mail, startled our elderly landlady beyond belief. My wife had watched our landlady open the door and tiptoe into our apartment, obviously to perfect the fine art of snooping. Spying, while reprehensible, isn't unusual and you should be aware of it. You must either take precautions to protect your privacy or realize that you run the risk of such a snoop sharing or disclosing information she discovers.

Disclosures of information secured by snoops can adversely affect you in many ways, including your standing and reputation in the community. If the information is incriminating, it can be turned over to the police. While the landlord may not admit the police to your apartment, the police may accept and use in court any evidence given to them by a trespasser, provided the police didn't instigate the trespasser's illegal conduct. The Fourth Amendment only protects against intrusions by the state or government, not those by private citizens, although such intrusions may be grounds for a lawsuit against the snooper.

I share an apartment. Can my roommate allow the police to search without my permission?

You and your roommate have surrendered a certain amount of privacy to each other in order to share your apartment. Naturally, your privacy is more limited than it would be if you lived alone.

Each of you has authority to admit guests to your apartment, and it's likely that over time you'll each have guests whom the other doesn't like.

If a police officer comes to your apartment to search for evidence against you, your roommate may consent to a search. The roommate can't waive *your* right to privacy, but he can waive *his* right to privacy. Consequently, even if the officer has asked your permission to search and been refused, your roommate may validly consent to a search of the shared spaces of the apartment, such as the living room and kitchen.

However those parts of the apartment that are yours exclusively may not be searched on the roommate's okay. If you each have your own bedroom, the police may not assume that the roommate can authorize a search of your room. Even in shared areas, you may have established exclusive use of certain cabinets and closets, and your roommate can't validly consent to a search of those areas. If a cabinet or closet is clearly marked as yours exclusively, the officers may not rely on your roommate's consent to search it.

I live at home. May my parents consent to a search of my room?

Ordinarily, the law presumes that parents may agree to a search of their entire home, even including their children's rooms. However, with the number of adult children remaining or returning to their parents' home to live, that presumption is not necessarily fair. Many parents and adult children have arrangements which aren't altogether different from those at a rooming house, involving payment of rent and respect for privacy. Nonetheless, police may ordinarily search the adult child's room based on the parents' consent, unless the officers know or should know that the parents don't actually have the authority to consent. Perhaps the economic situation which has resulted in more children living at or returning home may eventually lead courts to realize that all children, but especially adult children, are given certain privacy rights even within their own parents' home, and that it is unreasonable to allow police officers to assume that parents automatically have authority to consent to a breach of that privacy.

Searching with or without a warrant

What does a search warrant allow a police officer to do?

Issued by a judge, a search warrant orders police to search a specific address for specified evidence of a particular crime. A search warrant is issued when the police present a sworn statement containing sufficient facts and circumstances to persuade the judge that a crime has been committed, and that particular evidence of that crime will be found at the place to be searched.

The search warrant authorizes the police intrusion onto the premises, but it also limits the scope of their search. The warrant must contain a specific description or listing of the items to be searched for, instead of allowing a general exploratory search for any evidence. The officers may look anywhere on the premises where the items sought could be hidden. They may not look in other places. For example, a police officer executing a warrant ordering him to search for a stolen television set could only search in places where the television set might be hidden. As a result, the officer couldn't look into the bathroom medicine cabinet, a nightstand table (unless the television set was a watchman), or a film canister. On the other hand, if the only item specified in the warrant is a diamond ring, the officer could search virtually anywhere and in any container because the ring could be there.

Once the object sought is found, the search must end. If the ring were found in the first room searched, it would be improper for the police to continue to search in that or in any other room. If, however, while searching for the ring, the officer opened a canister in which the ring could be hidden and discovered other evidence of the original crime or evidence of a different crime, the officer could seize it. It must be immediately apparent, however, that the object is evidence of a crime. The officer may not examine the object or turn it over to check serial numbers.

At the completion of the search, the occupant must be provided with a complete list of anything taken by the police.

I've heard of police breaking in at night with a search warrant and rousting the sleeping occupants. Can they do that?

The situation you describe sounds more like police in other countries. However, the scenario is becoming more common here. Ordinarily, a search warrant must be executed during daylight hours. But if police demonstrate a reason why it's necessary to conduct the search at night, such as that the evidence is likely to be moved if they have to wait until the next day, a judge will authorize a nighttime search. Judges, these days, authorize night searches with little or no showing of necessity particularly in drug cases, where it is assumed that illegal drugs are always moved very quickly.

Does the requirement that an officer have a warrant to search my home apply to my backyard?

Your backyard is an extension of the living area of your home. Therefore, police are restricted from walking into your backyard and nosing around without a warrant, just as they would not be permitted into your home for that purpose.

The lay-out of most backyards, however, means that you will have less privacy than you would within your house. A backyard is generally open and visible to neighboring properties and the general public and the police may inspect or photograph whatever can be seen by the general public. If your hot tub is visible from your neighbors' windows, you can't complain when they look out and see you naked. Provided the police don't trespass into your backyard, they may look into it from any place to which they have lawful access. And remember, observation from an airplane is permissible without a warrant or cause, even if a specific backyard is targeted and police hover above that property in a helicopter!

When may police search my home without a warrant?

The Constitution aggressively guards your security in your home from invasion by police. Even the present Supreme Court continues to limit police entry into your home without a search warrant. However, the privacy interests protected by the search warrant requirement must give way when equal or more important interests are at stake. For example, no one would suggest that police should first get a search warrant to enter a home when there are calls for help coming from the home, or when neighbors report violence within a home.

An immediate danger of harm to someone, however, isn't the only recognized necessity that permits police to bypass a search warrant. If facts exist which lead police to believe that evidence of a serious crime will be destroyed or immediately removed from a location, police may act without a search warrant rather than risk losing that evidence by taking the time to get a warrant. The evidence may be challenged before it is used in a criminal case, and the police will have to establish the reasonableness of their belief that an emergency justified their search without a warrant.

Does that mean that a police officer who sees a marijuana plant growing in a window can enter without a warrant?

No, it doesn't, although the person who puts a marijuana plant in a window doesn't win a prize for intelligence. Because this isn't an emergency situation or one involving potential violence, the officer must obtain a search warrant. To do this, the officer must be lawfully present, and not trespassing, when he spots the plant. On the assumption that the officer is on the street or sidewalk when he spots the plant, his observation of the plant provides probable cause of illegal conduct, which is sufficient to obtain a warrant. It isn't *either* probable cause or a warrant which is necessary to enter to conduct a search, but *both*. Probable cause is needed for a court to issue a warrant. Many searches have been found illegal, especially searches of homes, where there is strong probable cause, but where police failed to secure a warrant. Only a necessity, along with probable cause, would justify a warrantless entry in the marijuana plant example. For instance, if the officer could show that you were aware of his observation of the plant, and thus could have destroyed it, a warrantless entry would be justified.

Noisy parties and fights

May a police officer come into my house when he comes to the door because of neighbors' complaints about a noisy party?

One of the common tasks we assign to police in our communities is to iron out neighborhood disagreements. While a complaint about a noisy party is unlikely to lead to true violence, the noise can be disturbing and irritating to others who are trying to sleep or enjoy other activities without unwanted noise disturbing their peace. When a police officer knocks on your door in response to a complaint about noise, the officer is trying to smooth over everyone's feelings. Before knocking on the door, the officer generally can gauge the level of noise.

It is unnecessary for the officer to enter your house or apartment just to seek a reduction in noise level. So it is completely up to you whether the officer may come in. Probably, the only reason the officer might request entry is to determine whether there are any underage people drinking or whether anyone is using an illegal substance. You are within your rights to refuse the officer's request. Just politely assure him that the noise

level will be kept at an acceptable level. If you consent
to the officer's entry of the house, then he may take
action if he sees any violations of the law. Again, your
permission to enter doesn't give him permission to
search the whole house. Without indication of a real
problem, there's really no justification for the officer
wandering beyond your front room nor may he search
your effects or look into drawers or closets, even in that
room.

You can't ignore reasonable requests to stop disturbing other people, however. If the disturbance continues, despite police requests to stop, it would be
appropriate for the officer to enter and to arrest people
who are disturbing the peace.

This is such a common friction point between
police and young people that a few rules of common
sense can take you out of the danger zone. When a
police officer alerts you that your party is spilling over
and the noise is bothersome to others, simply take
action and quiet things down, so that the officer doesn't
have to come back. You are on notice that the police are
aware of your party and will keep an ear open for any
further disturbance. If they do return, don't voluntarily
admit the police officer to the party, unless you are sure
of the age of everyone who might be drinking and are
confident that no illegal substances are being used. If
the police officer insists on entering, don't resist. Make
sure, however, that someone else at the party observes
that the officer came in without your consent.

**You mean a police officer can just come into my house to
arrest me or someone who is there?**

A police officer may not ordinarily enter without
consent to arrest a resident without an arrest warrant—
an order from a judge to make an arrest. Like a search
warrant, an arrest warrant may be issued only if the
police have probable cause, based on sufficient facts, to
believe that a crime has been committed, and that it

has been committed by the person the police want to arrest. Moreover, a police officer needs a search warrant to enter a residence to look for and arrest a nonresident, unless there is an emergency or a resident consents to the search.

A warrantless entry to arrest without consent is permissible only if there are "exigent circumstances" (a necessity) that justify immediate action. Whether a claim of necessity is supportable will be determined by the seriousness of the offense, the likelihood of the person escaping if immediate action is not taken, and whether the person is armed and others might be in danger. The claim of exigent circumstances is stronger if the offense is dangerous, and officers believe that the person to be arrested is armed and others are present.

Now, you're right; this doesn't describe a noisy party. However, a police officer has the authority to stop an ongoing disturbance of the peace and especially to enter and do so when revelers ignore the officer's warnings. You and your guests have the opportunity to avoid both the arrest and the officer's entry to arrest. Failure to bring the party into compliance with the law's requirements, and to stop creating a public disturbance, puts you and your guests at risk of both arrest and the officer's entry to make the arrest, with the accompanying authority to seize any evidence in plain view. Even if disturbing the peace isn't an arrestable offense where you live, you're subject to arrest everywhere if you don't stop the illegal conduct after a request or warning to do so.

My friend was arrested right outside of the open door to his house for shooting off illegal fireworks. While he was being arrested, a second police officer walked inside the house and found several of his friends drinking beer. Could he arrest them for underage drinking as he threatened to do?

The officer probably would have arrested them, but she knew she risked embarrassment when their lawyers later challenged her right to be in the house. An

open doorway is not an open-ended invitation for anyone to enter. Su casa is *not* her casa. The officer had no
right to simply walk in to look around. Presumably, she
expected to find and confiscate the rest of the fireworks
right inside the door. When she found people violating
the liquor law, she was probably as surprised as they
were. Because she wasn't lawfully present, the evidence
she seized wouldn't be admissible in a juvenile or criminal proceeding, nor could she testify about what she
observed. As a result, there was no admissible evidence
to use against the young drinkers and they couldn't be
convicted.

If the youths had been outside when the fireworks
were being shot off and the officer observed them drinking, she could have arrested them and confiscated the
evidence. Then they would have been subject to conviction because the evidence and the officer's testimony
about what she saw could have been used at trial. Similarly, if the officer had not entered your friend's apartment, but first observed the drinking from outside the
open door, she could have entered and arrested the
drinkers and seized the evidence which was in plain
view. That's all she could have done; she couldn't have
searched any further into the house for additional
evidence.

**My roommate and I were having a very noisy, violent fight
and someone called the police. A police officer came to the
door after we had quieted down, but he insisted on coming in
even though my roommate told him everything was okay.
Could he do that?**

Not only did the circumstances allow for the officer
to come in, but if you think about it, you would have
approved of his decision to come into your house. A
situation like this could lead to a real tragedy if the
officer were to simply accept the assurance of the person who answers the door, without checking to see
whether someone inside is in danger. What if *you* were
in danger, and the officer left the scene without investi-

gating further, after being told that there was no problem?

The officer was dispatched to investigate a "noisy," "violent" fight. If you described the situation this way, imagine what it sounded like to your neighbors and what they told the officer, who was obliged to make sure that you were all right. However, after determining that no one was injured or in danger, the officer had no further authority to remain in your house and should have left immediately.

The same thing is true when police respond to a 911 call made by children playing with a telephone. A responding police officer can't accept a parent's assurance that nothing is wrong. The officer may enter and look through the house to make sure that no one is in danger, and that the child is okay.

Keep in mind that, once in the house, the officer need not act as though he is oblivious to objects which are in plain view, while he is making sure that no one needs assistance. If he sees a gun or contraband while talking with you or looking for you, he is entitled to seize it. The officer may not go rummaging through the house, however, except for the purpose which justified his entry.

Domestic disputes

My husband and I were fighting, and he struck me. I was so angry that I called the police. When they arrived, I calmed down and told them that I did not want to press charges. They arrested my husband anyway. Wasn't it up to me whether he got arrested?

Domestic violence is a major problem in this country. It cuts across age, gender, race, ethnic groups, and class lines. It is not limited to married persons. The law has awakened to the seriousness of this issue. In many states, domestic violence is a separate crime and, in some, second offenses are felonies.

The officer's first obligations are to make sure that no one is in danger, and to assure that no one *will* be in danger after she leaves. The immediate, fool-proof measure to ensure that no one will be seriously hurt in the ensuing hours is to separate the combatants. Generally, the only way to actually separate the parties is to arrest the one who has assaulted the other. Most often that will be the husband, but times are changing, and women are battering their partners with greater frequency.

Even if my husband gets arrested, isn't it up to me whether the case ever gets to court?

Following your husband's arrest, the police and the prosecutor will have to include you in their decision whether to actually prosecute your husband. He can't be convicted without your testimony, unless others saw him hitting you.

In some communities, prosecutors automatically accept the wife's decision not to prosecute and dismiss the charges. While this leaves the wife in control of the decision to proceed, not all authorities agree with this policy. Some experts feel that the community has an obligation to intervene and pressure the wife into testifying.

This can be accomplished by bringing legal pressure to bear on the wife. The prosecutor can request a subpoena, forcing the wife to testify even if she doesn't want to. In one community, a prosecutor sends a police car out to pick up the wife if she fails to show up on the day of her husband's scheduled trial. Generally, just the threat of this type of pressure is enough to get a reluctant-to-prosecute wife to cooperate. However, if her refusal results from her husband's threats she is placed in an intolerable situation. One can also see that legal pressure to testify might make the situation even worse for the wife because it prevents her from using the threat of criminal prosecution as leverage against her husband, often leaving her in a more vulnerable position within the already strained relationship.

On the other hand, if yours is an area where the authorities leave the decision to prosecute up to the wife, and you decline to do so, keep in mind that, if your husband hits you again, police and prosecutors may take you less seriously and be less enthusiastic about your case. Moreover, if your husband hits you and gets away with it once, he may feel that he can abuse you at will, without fear of legal consequences.

If your spouse or partner is battering you, you both need help. Please get it. First, there are shelters available to you so you can get out of the house. The police or a hospital can provide you with the name and telephone number of an organization that can give you this emergency assistance. In many communities, these shelters can provide more than just one or two night's housing, and your presence there, as well as the shelter's location, is kept confidential. They are linked to other social service agencies to help you get on your feet, find a job, find permanent housing, and get counseling.

Even if you don't want out, you and your spouse need help to turn the relationship around. Violence is not a normal part of a healthy relationship, and you shouldn't accept it. Don't feel that you are "trapped" or have no choice in the matter. You both need to discuss your situation with an expert. Such counseling is available in most communities. Call a free clinic, battered women's shelter, or a mental health referral service to find out what options exist in your community. This isn't only true in a conventional situation where a husband batters a wife, but in any relationship where there is violence.

Entry by building inspectors and other government officials

We have building inspectors where I live who come around and ask to come in the house. Can I say no?

The Fourth Amendment limits and regulates the authority of *government* to intrude on your privacy, and this doesn't just mean the police. Therefore, your right to be free from unreasonable searches and seizures applies to building inspectors, too.

Most communities set minimal health and safety standards in all residences, or at least rental units. These standards are enforced by periodic inspections to determine if the requirements are being met. You have an absolute right to refuse to permit an inspector to enter without a warrant.

A homeowner or tenant may consent to an inspector's request to enter, and no warrant is necessary until entry is refused. Keep in mind that an inspector who is conducting a lawful inspection, either with your consent or a warrant, may see other things which are visible to him as he goes about his duties and may legitimately report on what he sees to police or other officials.

The type of warrant needed for a health and safety inspection is easier to obtain than a warrant which police need to conduct a search for evidence of a crime. A showing that it is time for a periodic inspection generally results in issuance of such a warrant. However, the inspection must be legitimate and not merely a pretext to look around for criminal evidence on behalf of the police. Once a warrant has been obtained, failure to admit the inspector will lead to criminal prosecution.

Since a warrant for a building inspection is easily obtained, are there any benefits to requiring the inspector to obtain one?

There is always value in requiring public officials to obtain warrants. If nothing else, it ensures that the inspector seeks entry for a legitimate purpose and not for something other than what he tells you. A warrant assures you that the law requires an inspection, and that it is time for your dwelling to be inspected.

Most importantly, the building or health code sets the limits on the scope of the inspection. A code that requires periodic inspections to ensure that electric wiring is safe would authorize an inspector to look throughout a dwelling to make sure that wiring is not frayed or dangerous. It would not require the inspector to look into areas, such as an unlighted closet, where there is no wiring.

I have to apply for ADC assistance for my child. Can they come into my house to determine if I'm eligible?

Aid to Dependent Children funnels support through state programs to children in need, where the need exists because of the death or continued absence from the home of a parent, the incapacity of a parent, or the unemployment of a parent who makes the effort required by state law to find work. Home visits to determine initial and continued eligibility have been a touchy issue for a generation.

The law varies depending on where you live and your state's laws on the subject. Some states don't provide for home visits at all. Eligibility is determined on the basis of an application submitted at the agency. Some state laws which require home visits have been invalidated by state courts. Other states require initial home visits, and still others require initial and then periodic home visits. The purpose of these visits is plain. Where the application for aid is based on the absence of a father from the home, the visit is to assure that no able-bodied man resides in the home.

Where a home visit is required, you have the option to consent to the social worker's inspection. However, if you refuse to permit the inspection, the application for aid *may* be denied or existing aid *may* be terminated. The United States Supreme Court upheld a state law which denied future benefits when an applicant refused to allow a social worker to make a home visit.

These requirements have been under attack in many states, with varying outcomes, resulting in a veritable patchwork of different regulations. Some states maintain an active visit requirement, terminating aid on refusal. Another requires a second attempt to visit, with prior notice, before refusal may result in the termination of benefits. A third state allows an applicant to refuse a home visit, even if there is prior notice, without termination of aid, if the applicant is willing to visit with the caseworker elsewhere. Another state court ordered agencies within that state to terminate all home visits.

As you can see, it is impossible to tell you what to expect in your own state. Your best bet is to call the local Legal Aid Society for information on the home visit requirement in your community.

Can child welfare investigators make home visits?

Social service agencies charged with monitoring the welfare of children may act when they receive reports from teachers, neighbors, hospitals, or other sources about neglect or mistreatment of a child. A social service agency which acts on the basis of a report of abuse or neglect may consider it necessary to visit the home and inspect the child's home environment.

Typically, a case worker will come to the home first and seek consent for a home visit. You have an absolute

right to refuse consent to this intrusion. There will be
no adverse consequences from the refusal, nor will it
result in termination of benefits.

Following refusal, the agency can gain admission
only by securing a search warrant from a judge. A warrant will be issued only on presentation of substantial
evidence that demonstrates the need to search the
child's environment. A search warrant will specify what
they are looking for, limiting the scope of the search.
Only in rare instances, where an emergency exists and
the child is in immediate danger, would social service
agencies be empowered to enter, probably with the
assistance of the police, without consent or a warrant.

Landlords and eviction

**Can my landlord enter my apartment in order to remove my
possessions and evict me?**

You really don't have too much to worry about if
you're meeting the conditions of your lease. An eviction
terminates the tenant's right to occupy rented premises. Eviction is permitted in a situation where there is
no lease (known as a month-to-month tenancy) when,
after the landlord has given proper notice of intent to
terminate the relationship, the tenant fails to move out
at the end of a month. In the case of a lease, a landlord
can evict a tenant if he fails to honor any of the
promises made in the lease. The most common reason
for eviction is the failure to pay rent. The duty to pay
rent is a built-in part of the landlord-tenant relationship, and the landlord may evict the tenant and terminate the lease if the rent is not paid.

A landlord may not evict a tenant to retaliate for
the tenant complaining to a government agency or otherwise taking action concerning the landlord's failure to
comply with the promises that the landlord made in the
lease. A landlord's failure to make necessary repairs or
live up to the terms of the lease doesn't mean that you

can simply stop paying rent. Most states require that, to avoid eviction, you must deposit the rent with a housing court.

There are three approaches to eviction. Traditionally, a landlord, using "self-help," could simply reoccupy the rented property on the tenant's default under the lease. However, self-help always contains a potential for violence and injury. In order to get away from that potential, most states have enacted laws requiring the landlord to obtain a court order. Some states prohibit self-help and allow eviction only if the landlord takes the required legal steps, with court approval. Others allow self-help, provided it is limited to peaceful entry with a passkey, otherwise requiring the landlord to go to court.

The eviction laws are meant to allow landlords to regain possession of property after giving a tenant notice (generally three days) to vacate. The tenant is informed that if he doesn't move out, the landlord will file an eviction action, which is a civil proceeding in court. Although this proceeding is intended to lead speedily to trial, without all of the formalities which govern most trials, "speedy" is used in the legal sense, and you will be provided at least a few days to prepare for the trial or to move. If the landlord wins the eviction action, the court will order you to vacate the premises. You will ordinarily be given a week or more to do so. If you fail to do so, your possessions will be removed, and you will be denied further entry.

Occasionally, the shoe is on the other foot, and you want out of a lease because the landlord has failed to provide you with livable conditions. Those conditions are, for example, adequate heat and the making of promised or necessary repairs. Ordinarily, you would be concerned that, if you move out, the landlord will still require you to pay rent under the lease. It is called a *constructive* eviction when the landlord makes an apartment or house unsuitable for occupancy. The tenant must move out because the apartment is not fit to live in. In this case, if the landlord sues for the rent, the tenant can defend on the basis of the constructive eviction. The tenant may be entitled to collect damages from the landlord to cover the costs of moving and the additional rent if the replacement apartment is more expensive.

5 ON CAMPUS

Notwithstanding the movies' vision of college life as an undisturbed playland, sometimes that idyll is harshly interrupted by legal problems. Many of those problems are universal and are treated in other chapters of this book. Some, however, are peculiar to college students, like dorm searches and challenging academic and disciplinary expulsions. Others, like sexual harassment, while relevant in the work place, too, seem to be particular problems on campus.

The status of being a college student is not the equivalent of having no rights or recourse. You do have rights and remedies, as well as responsibilities.

Dorm room searches

I returned from class and found a Resident Assistant in my dorm room holding a can of beer he found there. I turned red, and then white with fear, but noticed he did, too. I haven't heard anything about it since. Can you tell me why this happened?

A generation ago, RAs at state, as well as private, colleges and universities regularly inspected dorm rooms for violations of law and university rules. It is amazing to look back on it and realize how RAs entered rooms without any consideration for the residents' privacy. Perhaps most shocking is that it was accepted without question. Moreover, residence hall personnel made periodic inspections to make sure that students did not have prohibited appliances in the dorms—the same electrical appliances that are common in dorms today.

What happened in your situation is that you caught the RA red-handed, breaking the rules which govern his conduct, while he was discovering evidence that you broke the university's rules.

What has changed over the course of the last generation is how dormitory rooms are viewed, and how the relationship between students and university officials is defined. In the past, a dormitory room was looked on as similar to a bedroom in a parent's house. The parent or parent substitute could enter at will to make sure that the student was following the house rules. That took an unrealistic view of the rental arrangement and the relationship between a student and university officials.

The arrangement today is based on a more realistic understanding: college students are mostly over the age of majority, have increasing independence in their affairs, and must pay the consequences of their actions. For all practical purposes, a student's dorm room is his home. A student is reasonable to expect privacy there, including freedom from arbitrary and unreasonable intrusions into that living space. At least at state colleges and universities, the Bill of Rights works to help shape and enforce that expectation.

In a manner of speaking, the university is a landlord. If you start with a landlord-tenant relationship, you understand that a landlord cannot enter a tenant's apartment whenever he wants. At the same time, the nature of a college or university dormitory requires some change of the limits placed on a landlord. There are special needs in the university setting and in the college-student relationship. University employees are not held to the same standards as a landlord, since the university is obligated to protect campus order and discipline and promote an atmosphere consistent with its educational mission. It is important to balance a student's need for privacy and the university's special needs and responsibilities.

So if a dorm resident is different from a tenant, when can an RA legally go into my room without my permission?

State universities instruct dorm residents and RAs on the terms and conditions under which RAs may enter dorm rooms to investigate misconduct. Students are notified at the beginning of the school year of these policies. Residents would be wise to pay attention to these guidelines and any other terms and conditions specified in housing contracts. Universities are concerned with keeping harmonious conditions in dorms by preventing RAs from being heavy-handed and intrusive. They also want to prevent lawsuits based on illegal intrusions into dorm rooms.

Generally RAs are instructed that they must have a reasonable suspicion that a student resident is violating the school's disciplinary rules before entering a dorm room to investigate. Reasonable suspicion means just that: a suggestion of wrongdoing raised by actual occurrences or circumstances, and not simply unsupported feelings or hunches. If you recall, reasonable suspicion is the legal basis required for a police officer to stop your car or to stop you on foot. It is a less demanding standard than probable cause, which we talked about as the requirement for an arrest or search warrant. To show probable cause, the RA who investigated must present sufficient facts to show that it was reasonable for him to believe that misconduct was probably taking place, rather than his simply having reason to suspect it.

While reasonable suspicion appears to be the prevailing standard, some courts and commentators argue that the stricter standard of probable cause should govern entry into living quarters. Even though a university has authority to control its educational setting, there is nothing about the educational setting that justifies granting a university greater power to search a dorm room than would exist in any other housing arrangement. This argument appears strongest when the search is conducted for contraband or instruments or tools of crime, such as marijuana, which could be used in disciplinary proceedings that are similar to criminal proceedings. One lawsuit brought by students against state college officials even resulted in the court's stating that probable cause, the stricter standard, and a *warrant* issued by a court are necessary, unless an emergency requires the college or dormitory officials to enter and search a student's room.

When can I realistically expect an RA to enter or search my room, and what will happen if something improper or illegal is found?

In light of the law's uncertainty, it is not at all surprising that most public colleges and universities play it very conservatively when it comes to entering and searching a student's dormitory room. RAs are instructed, under most circumstances, to knock on the dorm room door and obtain the student's consent before entering. Note that your voluntary consent is always sufficient authority for entrance and a search, regardless of whether there is suspicion or probable cause. However, consent for the police to enter *is not*, by itself, a consent to search. Where a dorm room is shared, either roommate may consent to the entry and search of the room and her own possessions. It would not be reasonable for an official, however, to rely on one roommate's consent to search the other's possessions.

Most schools instruct RAs not to unlock the door of the dorm room without the resident's consent. Naturally, these restrictions don't apply any time there is danger or a life-threatening emergency. When a student refuses admittance, the RA usually turns the matter over to the professional residence life staff. The staff then decides whether to enter without the student's permission, bring in the police to search the room, or merely file a report for future use, depending on the nature of the suspected violation and the resident's disciplinary history. Discretion is typically vested in the professional staff.

Once residence hall employees discover evidence of misconduct, a student can expect some kind of disciplinary response from the residence life staff. The response may range from an informal discussion with the student's RA or Senior Residence Advisor to a hearing before a disciplinary board, which may result in eviction for violation of the residence hall lease, or suspension or expulsion from the college or university. Of course, if evidence of illegal conduct is found, it may be turned over to the police.

May the college or university let police search my dormitory room?

Even in states where college and university officials may search a dormitory room without a student's consent, that authority does not automatically extend to admitting police to search. A dormitory room is no different from a house or apartment when it comes to police entering to search. Our society guarantees us the greatest protection of privacy in our homes from police or other governmental intrusion. It doesn't matter whether that home is a grand mansion, a rundown shack, or a dormitory room.

Except in an emergency situation, university officials may not admit police to a dormitory room. Instead, the same conditions apply as would to entry of a different type of residence. Absent an emergency, police must have probable cause and a search warrant to enter and conduct a search, or the permission of the resident. The university's consent is not the same as the resident's consent. Even if the university claims that a resident in a housing contract has impliedly consented to the university entering his room, that consent is given to the university, not to the police. The university should not be permitted to transfer or delegate that authority.

At our school, college officials show up unannounced and uninvited to dorm and fraternity parties to make sure that campus rules on drinking are enforced. Can we stop them?

Probably not. What university officials are doing is what they have been doing for generations, only now with a new emphasis. Underage and excessive drinking at campus parties is looked upon more seriously now than it once was. Historically, it was viewed only as a legal issue. Now, along with the legal issue, these matters are recognized for the health and safety issues they pose, and thus the university's concern and involvement are even more justified. Parents and politicians, alike, expect the resulting intrusiveness. Besides the health issues, there are basic safety issues as well. Students who drink excessively at campus parties often drive and are a danger to themselves and others on the road. Moreover, most claims of gang rape on campus seem connected to parties and excessive drinking. In fact, the pendulum is swinging toward stricter enforcement in the immediate future, rather than a more relaxed attitude.

Parties taking place in university dorms, which are university property, are subject to university rules and regulations. Greek houses, even if privately owned, are chartered on campus and thus subject to the school's rules pertaining to conduct and the consumption of alcohol. The university has the authority to enforce its rules in both types of facilities. Assistant deans dropping in on parties is a classic means of enforcement. Your complaints will fall on deaf ears within the university, and you will receive no more sympathetic hearing in a court of law.

I'm in high school, but I wonder if I can sneak in a question here. In my school, teachers and principals have been regularly searching lockers. That sounds contrary to what you have been saying. Can they do that?

A search of a high school student's locker is not at all the same as a search of a dormitory room. You have a constitutional right, even in high school, to be free from unreasonable searches and seizures. However, what is considered "reasonable" is viewed differently when it's a locker being searched as opposed to a dorm room which is accorded the safeguards given a home.

A locker inspection policy, nonetheless, must meet the reasonableness requirement. One can hardly argue that the presence of weapons, drugs, and alcohol on school premises does not present a hazard to other students and teachers and seriously detract from the learning environment. Therefore, the school may undertake reasonable steps to remove these objects from the school. Accordingly, an inspection policy directed towards that end will be upheld. Students and parents should be notified of the inspection policy, and procedures should be published within the school so that the inspections are not misused.

Different considerations apply when all lockers are to be inspected or when a particular student's locker and possessions are to be searched. While a general policy of inspecting all lockers will not violate the constitution, singling out one student and searching her locker or possessions requires a reasonable suspicion that contraband or prohibited items will be found in the locker. Remember, reasonable suspicion must be based on facts and circumstances, not hunches.

Disciplinary hearings

What can I expect at a college disciplinary hearing?

At a state college or university, constitutional notions of fairness require at least notice and an opportunity for a hearing before a student is suspended or expelled. The university must give the student notice of the charges against him and, if the student denies the charges, an explanation of the evidence and an opportunity to present a defense. Naturally, the notice and hearing should be given to the student before suspension, unless the student poses such a threat to the school that he must be removed from campus immediately.

The fairly recent application of these procedural due process of law requirements to colleges and universities runs contrary to the traditional rule of deferring to the educational institution's judgement in matters of discipline. While deference has its place, college and university students need protection from arbitrary and discriminatory administrative rulings no less than anyone else in society, and perhaps more than many. Courts considering claims by students that they were treated unfairly will look to see, not whether the students were accorded the same procedures that they would have been in a court of law, but instead whether these minimal standards of fairness were followed. Beyond that, the court will be concerned that the college or university followed its own rules and procedures leading up to the discipline of the student, and that the decision was arrived at by an impartial tribunal.

At a private college or university, the law does not demand the same procedures or standard of fairness that it does of state colleges and universities. The reason is that constitutional principles of due process of law apply only to government institutions or entities, and thus only to state educational institutions. What type of proceeding you are guaranteed at a private college depends on the terms under which you accepted admission to the school. More and more private institutions, however, have recognized that decency dictates that they provide the same assurances of fairness to their students that students at a state institution receive, even if not required to do so by law.

Can evidence obtained when an RA illegally enters a dorm room be used in a disciplinary hearing?

Evidence is not admissible in a criminal case when it is obtained through the illegal conduct of a police officer or other state official or employee. Nonetheless, the general rule is that a university, in its disciplinary proceedings, may use evidence which was obtained illegally. A university student, therefore, should expect to undergo the normal disciplinary process, regardless of the manner in which the university discovered the evidence forming the basis of the disciplinary charges. The result is that the university has the right to punish the student for rule violations, even though it came upon the evidence by violating the student's constitutional rights, as well its own university policies. However, the potential for this outcome may be lessened by the fact that the student could file a civil suit against the school for violating his right to privacy.

Courts occasionally have come up with a different rule, when the university-imposed punishment is overly severe and greater than would have been imposed if criminal charges had been filed against the student for the same conduct. In those cases, it has been difficult for schools to maintain the general argument that a university disciplinary proceeding is unlike a criminal trial.

When will university officials turn over evidence found in a dorm room to the police?

This is a matter of school policy which obviously differ from school to school. Moreover, colleges and universities are not keen on disclosing this policy, preferring instead to dangle the possibility over the violator's head.

However, a few examples can be cited. At the University of Virginia, "student self-government" is emphasized and violations of alcohol and drug laws are generally reported to university disciplinary bodies, while other infractions are dealt with on a case-by-case basis. Nonetheless, senior residence advisors are instructed to use their judgment as to whether to begin school disciplinary proceedings, call the police, or both.

A student with no history of misconduct who is found
in possession of marijuana is likely only to have the
incident recorded in her file and to face a discussion
with a senior staff member. At the University of Texas,
on the other hand, campus police are automatically
called if the resident is found violating drug laws, but
not if the resident is drinking underage. At the University of Michigan, RAs are instructed not to be too quick
to call Ann Arbor police because local courts have been
reluctant to get involved in what they consider university disciplinary matters.

Obviously these are not hard and fast rules. The
more serious the violation, the more likely the police
will be called in, as they should be. The public would
be outraged to think that university students are not
being prosecuted for serious criminal violations. However, what is deemed a serious criminal violation may
depend on the amount of publicity attracted by a particular incident and the pressure brought to bear on the
university.

In trouble off campus

**I loaned my student ID to my roommate who was going drink-
ing. He was arrested for underage drinking and *my* ID was
confiscated. Can I get in trouble?**

If the state can prove that you gave your roommate
your ID knowing and intending that he was going to use
it to gain entrance to a bar and be served alcohol illegally, you could be in serious trouble. You have aided
and abetted your roommate's commission of a crime.
There is a difference, though, between merely facilitat-
ing his commission of the crime, and aiding and abet-
ting, which requires that you *intended* to assist him in
the commission of the crime or, at the least, that you
knew that he was going to use your ID illegally. To be
guilty of the crime, depending on the relevant state law,
the state would have to prove beyond a reasonable

doubt that you intended the outcome, or at least that you knew the likelihood of the outcome.

They can only prove these matters, however, if you or your roommate volunteer the information. Where a student is caught using someone else's ID, as opposed to a purchased, false ID, the authorities assume that the owner gave it to the student, but rarely proceed against the owner because of the difficulty of securing proof. The college or university will likely have a different standard, and you may face disciplinary proceedings.

As a prank, I stole a napkin dispenser from a fast food hamburger spot off campus, and now all hell has broken loose. First, I was arrested. Isn't this an over-reaction?

One person's prank is another's crime. You might be surprised how common it is for simple, harmless college pranks that backfire to be treated as criminal acts by local authorities. These so-called pranks end up resulting in criminal charges most commonly for theft, trespass, destruction of property, and disorderly conduct. All are misdemeanors, but all will probably result in a criminal record and could result in jail sentences, although a jail sentence for a first misdemeanor offense is not likely.

You shouldn't be shocked at the reaction either of the fast food establishment or of the town police. Business people view theft as a major problem and are not going to be dissuaded from prosecuting just because it is only a five or ten dollar item. Local police are not going to attempt to talk local merchants out of filing charges, and will be guided by the merchant's decision as to whether to proceed. While many within a university community may view student pranks that do not get too out of hand with a merciful "students will be students" attitude, local police do not often share that view. Neither would you in their situation. In college towns, students make most of the work for police. The police don't understand that many or most students are

trying to make ends meet; instead, they see students as
spoiled kids with opportunities they (the police) didn't
have. Don't look to the police to cut you any slack, and
try not to give them the opportunity to classify you as
an antagonist.

Your description of what happened clearly fits the
definition of theft. You intended to permanently
deprive the owner of his property. It doesn't matter that
the object is worth only a few dollars; nor does it matter
that you had no ill will towards the owner of the property. Once you are past the age of eighteen, you may be
charged as an adult. Obviously, they didn't have to
charge you. The owner of the property could have
elected not to press charges, or the police or prosecutor
could have decided that there were too many other more
important matters on which to focus. But it is their
decision, not yours. By committing the foolish act, you
subjected yourself to their discretion.

**If I am convicted, can the conviction be used to deny me
future opportunities?**

As a youngster in school, you were probably
warned that certain conduct would go on your *permanent record*. This is what was meant by that record. But
even here, its consequences need not be catastrophic.
After a period of time set by statute, a misdemeanor
conviction may be expunged on a petition filed in the
court where the charge was heard. Expungement is a
sealing of the records of the case, so that they cannot be
accessed by employers or others checking on your past
history. In most states, however, expungement is only
available if the offense is the only one on the record.

Even if it cannot be expunged, the damage can be
controlled and limited. A conviction of this nature is
not likely to keep you out of graduate or professional
school, keep you from practicing law, or even keep you
out of the armed forces. You will have to explain it and
demonstrate, by having no subsequent arrests and con-

victions, that it was a youthful indiscretion. Most people have had brushes with the law and are more sympathetic than the police. Just don't make a habit of such conduct, because the sympathy will dry up quickly.

OK, so far. I pled "no contest" on the advice of an attorney and was fined. Now, however, I have received notice to report to the Dean of Students' office to answer internal charges related to the theft. Didn't my court appearance put an end to the case?

Once was a time when that notice would have been preparatory to your expulsion from the university. Times have changed, but not all that much. At times it has worked the other way, and students have been exempt from criminal prosecution for off-campus behavior, being subject only to the punishment determined by the school.

Your school undoubtedly is involved in a cooperative agreement with the local police department. Often that agreement is between the municipal and campus police departments. The school is notified following the arrest of one of its students. Sometimes that is done so that someone may arrange bail. Sometimes, as here, it is for disciplinary reasons.

You are very unlikely to be expelled for your high jinks. Nonetheless, a state or private college or university may discipline students for *any* behavior that is reasonably related to the school's educational mission. This authority extends to off-campus behavior. Institutions of higher education have been afforded a unique role within society, and courts will not examine college administrative decisions as closely as they would those of other institutions. Colleges and universities have been granted broad authority to decide what kinds of behavior affect their educational missions, *including behavior which demonstrates a lack of respect for rules.*

A legal challenge to a college's administrative decision to discipline a student for illegal behavior or conduct that violates school rules will generally fail, so long as the school can demonstrate any relationship between the violation and the school's mission. The school must also show that it used some type of procedure that allowed the student an opportunity to contest the charge. Ordinarily, that procedure need not be a formal hearing.

Courts traditionally yield to the school's decision, reasoning that one who is granted special privileges, such as the right to attend an institution of higher education, may be required to possess and exhibit superior standards of conduct, which may be set by the institution. Thus, the courts usually uphold institutional disciplinary action taken against students for off-campus drug use because of the possibility of the student affecting the learning environment at the college, and because of possible danger to other students in the institution. However, university disciplinary action taken against students for less serious conduct has also been upheld. For example, a court upheld a Pennsylvania college's suspension of a student, following a hearing, for entering a private, off-campus party to which he was not invited.

Flunking out

I flunked out. What's the likelihood of a court helping me get back in school if I sue?

Courts will intervene in this situation even more rarely than they will with college and university disciplinary proceedings. Traditionally, courts have deferred to a university's judgment on academic competence, believing that it is not a court's place to substitute its views for the historic judgment of academic experts. Furthermore, courts have noted that the educational process is not adversarial in nature, and that academic evaluations are different in character from judicial and administrative fact-finding proceedings.

Nonetheless, a student is entitled to fair and clear notice of academic requirements. Though once a student is given reasonable notice of these expectations, the school's rules of dismissal need only be applied equally and without arbitrariness.

However, for a student who has been dismissed from a college or university for academic failure, the process can be very adversarial. As a result, courts have become a bit more willing to provide minimal review, not so much of the final decision, but of the process leading up to the decision. Hence, an academic regulation that provides a basis for a student's dismissal must be for a school-related purpose, and the regulation must employ reasonable means to achieve the purposes served.

Above all, a student has the right to be treated fairly in the administration of an academic matter. An examination of the fair treatment question includes consideration of the school's grading criteria and the type of review process used in deciding whether to dismiss the student. In a few cases, courts have extended the notion of fair treatment to include a review of the quality of education received prior to the decision to dismiss the student, although this is exceedingly rare.

A successful challenge to a college or university decision to dismiss a student for poor academic performance will not result from an argument that the student was misgraded, or that the university's judgment about the student's abilities was incorrect. Rather, a successful challenge must establish that the college or university acted arbitrarily, in bad faith, in an irregular or unprofessional manner, or unequally with regard to race or gender.

Dealing with campus police

Our campus police tend to be power crazy. Whenever a group of students seems to be having a good time on the

**street, the police swarm around, barking orders, and threaten-
ing arrest. Is there anything we can do to put a stop to this?**

Campus police operate under policies developed by
the university. Rather than confront the police, the
matter should be taken up with university administrators, beginning with the Dean of Students' office. It is
possible that the university is not aware how strictly its
policies are being enforced. Student input into the
development of these policies makes abundant sense.
An alternative proposal would be to recommend creation of a campus police review board made up of students, faculty, administrators, and campus police.
Although this proposal is unlikely to lead to actual
creation of the board, it will probably result in accept-
ance of student input into the development of policies.

You have certain rights to be free from interference, even in public and on campus. You have the right
to be on the street and to come and go, and to come and
stay, without being hassled. Just congregating on the
street should not subject you to police directives.

On the other hand, police, like anyone else, are
permitted to walk up to anyone and engage that person
in conversation. Of course, put this way, you don't have
to respond or join that conversation. Police rarely talk
to people that way, and your description of what is
happening on your campus does not lead me to think
that the police are engaging you in friendly chats. Anything more than polite conversation, which you can
ignore, must meet certain constitutional standards.
Police cannot give orders, demand identification, or
order people to scatter, without legal justification. The
same standards which govern police in the community
or in airports, also govern police conduct on campus.
Arbitrary interference without cause is illegal.

That said, however, it's possible that you are providing legal cause for the police conduct you describe.
Some campus police departments have reputations for

being heavy-handed, and if you give them cause they are swift to use their power. One department with such a reputation arrested a student for mooning and took him in handcuffs to the police station where he was booked, finger-printed, and then charged with disorderly conduct.

Your description of having a good time leaves a lot to the imagination. I doubt that even the most heavy-handed campus police are about to interrupt a Frisbee, football, or other type of game, or a quiet discussion. So what you are probably talking about is a good time with a certain amount of rowdiness. Definitions of the crime of Disorderly Conduct are so general that virtually any rowdy behavior in a public place can fit the description, and thus subject you to police interference. Nonetheless, a certain amount of rowdiness on a college campus is to be expected and tolerated without interruption by the police. These are matters to be discussed with university officials. It is better to raise these issues in general, outside of the context of an actual conflict.

I attended a concert at the university stadium and was patted down before I was permitted to enter. How can they do that?

You have touched on another area where we have consented to a surrender of some Fourth Amendment rights to be free from unreasonable searches and seizures in return for increased safety and greater security. Point-of-entry searches are conducted to ensure that bottles, cans, or other dangerous projectile-like objects are not brought into the facility. The purpose of the prohibition is to prevent injury from thrown items. Probably, the search is also an attempt to keep alcoholic beverages and drugs out of the facility. The purpose, here, is to control behavior and prevent underage drinking by prohibiting all alcohol and drugs, or by limiting consumption of alcohol to that sold within the facility.

Your rights depend on whether it is a private stadium or a public or state university facility. If you were
entering a state university facility, the pat-down was
probably illegal and subject to challenge; it would not,
however, be illegal at a private (or private university)
facility.

There are no Fourth Amendment rights applicable
to private facilities, again because the Fourth Amendment pertains only to intrusions by the state or government. When you enter a private auditorium or stadium,
the terms and conditions of your entry are determined
by the agreement that you entered into when you purchased your ticket. I realize that you did not contem-
plate that your ticket purchase involved anything more
than the right to attend a concert or sporting event, but
in fact you entered into a contract with the seller. The
terms and conditions of that contract affect your right
to attend the concert. They may include a pat-down
search of your outer clothing and a visual inspection of
any containers you are carrying to make sure that you
are not bringing bottles, cans, or illegal items like
drugs, weapons, or fireworks, into the facility.

Operators of a public stadium or auditorium,
including one owned by a state university, may impose
similar prohibitions on alcohol, illegal objects, and bottles and cans. They are not free, however, to use the
same techniques as those used by private facilities to
enforce the prohibition because Fourth Amendment
guarantees limit the conduct of state employees. Generally, courts have condoned point-of-entry searches of
public facilities, as long as the search does not include
a pat-down or frisk of the patrons and their
possessions.

Thus, courts have upheld purely visual, or "eye-
ball," searches at these facilities, while disallowing
searches by security guards which involve feeling hand-
bags and purses to determine their contents, placing
hands inside a patron's coat pockets, and patting down

outer clothing. These same courts have recommended that the facilities ban all packages, purses, and pocketbooks, or maintain check rooms where the objects can be stored. Patrons may be required to open all packages for a visual inspection. Those refusing may be denied entry.

Mandatory drug testing

I have heard that my state university is considering mandatory drug testing each semester. Can they do that?

Only if you let them. Mandatory drug testing, except for student athletes, cannot be performed across the board or on a random basis. Requiring a student to submit to a test for traces of drugs in his system can only be done if there is an individualized suspicion that the particular student is using drugs. Again, the type of suspicion required must be based on specific facts and circumstances. A college official's hunch or subjective assessment that a student dresses like, or associates with, "druggies" will not do. Any attempt to institute mandatory drug testing on less than legally sufficient grounds is a serious violation of fundamental constitutional rights and can be challenged.

What about athletes?

Apparently, the NCAA (the National Collegiate Athletic Association, the governing body of college sports) and colleges and universities have decided that intercollegiate athletes are not entitled to the same constitutional protections as non-athletes are. Moreover, the courts have sanctioned this type of discrimination. The purpose of drug testing of athletes is two-fold. First, there is an interest in eliminating all illegal drug use. Second, there is a particular interest in detecting and eliminating the use of performance-enhancing drugs, like steroids.

Beginning in 1992, all Division I, II, and III colleges and universities associated with the NCAA are required to have their student athletes sign a consent to be tested. Any student who refuses to sign the consent is ineligible to compete in athletics at any NCAA school.

The NCAA drug testing program now has become year-round. Student athletes participating in conference championships and all post-season bowl and championship competitions are subject to testing. In team sports, testing during the regular season is done on randomly selected players. In individual sports, the top finishers in each event are likely to be tested, as well as other participants who are randomly selected.

In addition, more and more schools are instituting their own programs that require student athletes to consent to drug testing by the school. Some test football players four times a year and other athletes on a less regular basis. Some schools that have no testing program require students to sign a statement expressing the athlete's understanding that the school does not test. The purpose of this approach is to prevent an athlete from such a school from complaining about the school's failure to test, if the athlete makes it to a championship competition and then fails the NCAA-required drug test.

Privacy of student records

Can my college release information from my files, such as my grades or a prior suspension, to prospective employers?

Federal law provides that any college or university receiving federal funds may not give out personal information about a student contained in the school's educational records without the student's consent. Personal information includes such things as name, parents' names, addresses, social security number, personal characteristics about the student, grades, disciplinary records, and a student athlete's drug test results. The college or university may release certain "directory" information, such as names and addresses, provided that students are given general notice of this practice prior to the release of such information.

At the same time, a student must have access to her own records, except for parents' financial information or confidential statements of recommendation to which the student has waived access.

The law permits some disclosures without the student's permission, such as the release of information to a teacher or administrator within the institution. Certain other exemptions exist for disclosure to various government agencies, and the law contains an "emergency" provision allowing the release of information to protect the health and safety of the student or others.

Sexual harassment

I am a female student in an uncomfortable position with a male professor who has suggested several times that we go out together. How do you suggest I handle this?

Sexual harassment is not only overt suggestions that a student will benefit if she has sexual relations with a professor, or that she will suffer if she does not. Any situation in which a professor places a student in an uncomfortable situation concerning sexual conduct, sexual comments, or pressure to engage in social contact is sexual harassment. In a close case, where the conduct may not rise to a claim of sexual harassment, the professor's conduct is, at the very least, unprofessional. Moreover, sexual harassment is not confined to male professors and female students. Today, it extends to every form and combination.

For a considerable period of time, colleges and universities looked the other way and hoped that charges of sexual harassment, as well as the underlying problem, would go away. Now, most colleges and universities are no longer ignoring the problem, and, in fact, have established procedures for handling such situations. They'd better, because a failure to act on these matters, or acting in bad faith, can expose the institution to liability.

Sexual harassment falls under the general classification of sex discrimination in federal regulations. A school receiving federal funds must create a grievance procedure for resolution of student complaints, including discrimination based on sex. Furthermore, the college is required to designate an individual charged with handling these complaints, and to publicize the name and telephone number of this person.

The law of sexual harassment has developed two classifications. The first is where a student is pressured into sexual activity. The second involves the maintenance of a "hostile" or "abusive" environment, such as where a teacher makes suggestive comments to a student. In addition, a "hostile" environment exists where the college or university fails to institute grievance procedures, and thereby indirectly "permits" the teacher to engage in sexual harassment.

Call the university ombudsman or the Dean of Students' office to find out the procedures which exist on your campus. Someone has been assigned the obligation of assisting students or staff making such complaints. Don't be concerned about losing control of the matter just because you talk with that person. Ultimately, you retain the power to proceed or not; they cannot do it without you. I would encourage you to proceed, for chances are that you are not this professor's first victim, and if you don't act it is likely that you won't be his last. I understand that it takes courage to act, but until the courage is found, the situation won't get better.

Is it difficult to prove the truth of a sexual harassment claim?

Just because your college or university has developed a system for handling sexual harassment complaints does not mean that you will be satisfied with the process or the outcome. Ordinarily, the claim of sexual harassment results from conduct that takes place privately. Consequently, there are usually no witnesses to the improper advances. Most commonly, there will be a factual dispute between the professor and the complaining student. The professor will claim that the matter never occurred, and that the student is acting maliciously or is dreaming. There's no doubt that false accusations are made, but because a student knows that maintaining such a charge is not a picnic, it's not a frequent occurrence.

Even where it is impossible to resolve the issue because it is one person's word against another's, colleges and universities maintain files of charges and the existence of prior complaints should help to strengthen a present or future charge. Repeated denials that improper advances were not made soon become unbelievable.

Alternatively, the professor may claim that the student misunderstood his comments. Of course, in this situation, the professor is admitting making the comments, and a fact finder can determine the propriety of those comments.

Obscene telephone callers and other harassers

I have received a series of telephone calls from a person who either makes obscene suggestions or just breathes hard into the phone. How can I stop this?

Most people who make obscene telephone calls have no idea how stupid and obnoxious they are. In most cases, it is a sorry, fantasy substitute for a real sex life. Primarily, these people are seeking a reaction from the recipient. So the best way to handle it is merely to hang up and not engage the caller in conversation or argument. Most callers tire quickly when ignored. Under no circumstances should you provide the caller with any information about yourself, especially your name or address. Just because the caller has your phone number does not mean that the caller knows your identity or address. If the person is really offensive, and you want to send your own message, blow a high-pitch whistle into the telephone.

If the caller persists, the telephone company and the police can assist you. It is, after all, a crime to make obscene or harassing telephone calls. First, the telephone company will change your number if you wish, and also has equipment that can identify the telephone numbers from which calls to your number are made. In this way, the identity of the caller can be determined if the calls are being made from the same business or residential telephone. You will be asked to keep a log of when you receive the obscene calls so that the log can be compared against calls identified as originating from those telephone numbers. When a match is made, that information is turned over to the police and you have the option of prosecuting the caller. The telephone company will activate that equipment on request from you or the police.

I live in an off-campus apartment with three other girls. We have received harassing calls from someone we do not know, and he also has made noises outside of our apartment. He even came into our apartment wearing a mask when one of my roommates was there and warned her against leaving the door unlocked. Although he eventually left, he wouldn't when she first demanded that he do so. How should we deal with this situation?

America's college campuses do not present the undisturbed safe haven that they did thirty years ago. The crime which pervades our society has crept into college towns and onto college campuses. It is not surprising because in any large group of people the law of averages dictates that there will be some of every kind, including criminals and perverts.

The situation you describe should not be taken lightly. While it is possible that the person harassing you and your roommates may turn out to be a harmless prankster, there are aspects of his conduct which are troubling and threatening. When he entered your apartment, he committed a crime. He trespassed on private property and refused to leave. Depending on the definition of the offenses in the state where you live, he might have committed the more serious crimes of breaking and entering or burglary. In any event, the seriousness of his conduct escalated when he demonstrated a willingness to do more than just annoy you on the telephone—which is itself a criminal offense. Your roommate was very lucky that he did nothing more than warn her.

You should respond to this matter and make sure that college authorities or local police do as well. You and your roommates should agree on a strategy for handling this. First, make sure that your door is locked at all times. He may not have comprehended the seriousness of his behavior when he entered through an unlocked door. Second, notify local and campus police and the Dean of Students' office. Third, follow up on this notice; do not let the police dismiss this fellow as a prankster. He may be a prankster, but his conduct is sufficiently troubling that he should be taken seriously. Request the dean's office to notify the police of their interest. Fourth, report any suspicious behavior around your apartment to the police. Fifth, make sure that when you are out at night, you do not return to your apartment alone. Have someone accompany you from the parking lot or bus. Sixth, notify your neighbors so that they, too, are on the lookout for suspicious behavior. Hopefully, this action will send the right message to your menacer and will discourage him from persisting. Finally, don't let down your guard. Living with

your guard up is not pleasant, but it is necessary in
your situation.

Campus crime

**I have lost bikes to thieves, even though I was taking adequate
steps to prevent such thefts. What can I do?**

Theft of bicycles on campus is a problem all over
the country. Mountain bikes are reportedly the most
common target, although theft of all bikes is on the rise.
Moreover, no lock is theft-proof. A u-shaped lock *with* a
sleeve provides the greatest protection, though it, too, is
not foolproof. There are other steps you can take to help
reduce the likelihood of your bike being a target. Participate in campus and municipal registration and
engraving efforts so that if your bike is stolen, it can be
identified. Moreover, the theft insurance guarantees of
many lock companies require registration. Use bike
racks in heavily trafficked areas, not those in out-of-
the-way locations. Even if it takes a thief just thirty
seconds to undo a lock, he will be deterred if there are
many people around.

You may be able to recover the value or part of the
value of the bike under your parents' homeowner's
insurance. Frequently, homeowner's insurance extends
to possessions of dependent children even though they
are away at school. In order to file a claim, you will need
a police report indicating that the theft was reported.
Your recovery under the policy could be the value of the
bike minus the deductible on the policy. If recovery is
provided under your parent's policy it extends to all of
your possessions up to the value indicated in the
policy.

Is a college or university ever liable for damages when a student, employee, or visitor to campus is a victim of crime on the campus?

In most situations where a person is a crime victim, no one but the criminal is responsible for what happened. However, a college or university has the duty to protect students, employees, and visitors from harm caused by the criminal conduct of others where the danger is reasonably foreseeable, and the acts of the school created the danger. Liability will depend on whether the institution was negligent in failing to take reasonable protective measures.

For example, a college or university is required to provide adequate security in dormitories and campus buildings. Adequate security does not mean a campus police officer or security guard on every floor. Such a requirement would be unreasonable. How much security is required, though, and how much was actually provided will help to draw the line between negligence and no liability.

In determining whether reasonable protective measures have been taken, the type and quality of locks on doors through which an intruder entered is very relevant. Similarly, an institution must take other reasonable protective measures. It may be negligent to let foliage grow wild in certain areas where to do so gives an attacker or intruder a place to hide, and thus creates an unreasonably dangerous condition. Likewise, inadequate lighting which does not allow a person to observe someone hiding may create culpability. Moreover, it may be negligent not to warn students about danger in particular areas of a campus.

In other words, an institution is not liable for damages simply because it was the scene of a crime. The question becomes whether the institution took the necessary steps that a reasonable institution would to protect people on campus. Campuses are not going to be crime free, but our exposure to crime can be reduced by precautionary steps taken by the college or university.

Proving the school's negligence is not the only difficulty when bringing a civil suit. A college or university may be immune from a suit for damages under state law. While such immunity has dwindled and been made subject to many conditions over the last two decades, it may still provide a barrier to a suit in your state. If you have been a victim of crime on campus and you think the college or university created a dangerous condition which led to the crime, consult a lawyer who will be able to advise you on the feasibility of suing successfully. This is the type of lawsuit that would be taken on a contingent fee basis which means that the lawyer gets paid only if you are awarded a judgment. The lawyer's fee is a percentage of the total judgment. In other words, if you don't win, it won't cost you.

Date rape

If I was raped on a date, will the fact that I willingly went on the date make it more difficult to prosecute the case?

Date or acquaintance rape is generally treated by the law no differently than rape by a stranger. Neither form of rape is better or less blameworthy than the other. Stranger rape often involves greater force than that which accompanies date rape, and injury to the victim may be more likely. Date rape, however, involves a breach of trust, and the psychological injury may be greater.

The definition of rape varies from state to state, although there are certain common patterns. Traditionally, rape meant sexual intercourse with a woman, not the wife of the defendant, by force and without her consent. Today, most state statutes have eliminated the requirement that the act be accompanied by force. The force requirement existed simply to prove that the woman had not consented. It is also rape to surreptitiously slip a woman alcohol or drugs to impair her judgment or self control in order to have sex. Some modern statutes have eliminated the marital exemption or made it inapplicable where the husband and wife are living apart. Other states have further modernized their laws by adopting gender-neutral statutes so that the defendant and victim may be of either or the same sex, and have extended the definition of rape to cover forced oral and anal sex.

The principal issue in a case like yours is whether you consented. In some states, even if you did not consent, your assailant would not be held responsible if a jury found that he believed that you had consented. Most of those states require that a reasonable person would have misperceived the situation as the accused did.

Will my background or relationship **other men be used to show I consented?**

A woman's consent inferred from the way she is dressed. Claim oman brought on an attack because she was ght shorts or a short skirt are outrageous a . Similarly, a woman's prior conduct is not r her behavior during the incident at issue. T at a woman consented to sexual intercourse r men, or even with the same man in th s not mean that she con- sented to sex a with the person in question. Most states ield" statutes preventing the introduction, in a rial, of the victim's past sexual conduct or sexual reputation. Every woman, from saint to prostitute, and for that matter every person, has the right to say "no."

There is no question that men and women still do not look upon the conduct leading to sexual intercourse in the same way. Men hear "no" but often read "yes" into other words and conduct. Women, on the other hand, feel that the statement "no" is self-explanatory, regardless of other conduct, and that a woman is free to engage in any other conduct leading up to sexual intercourse, having already firmly drawn the line. In this conflict, women clearly have the better argument. "No" should be accepted as just that. Any person who implies anything else from a clear statement acts at his own peril. If you think there are mixed signals, stop and clarify the situation or face the consequences. There can be little sympathy for the claim that one got "carried away."

While women have the better argument, that is no satisfaction following a violent attack. Moreover, women have to be aware that the world, including the justice system, does not always treat them fairly. In their own self-interests, women would be wise to make sure that they are not sending mixed signals, and that their partners are not perceiving mixed signals. Mixed signals most often are sent and perceived when the parties are using drugs and alcohol. Moderation in the use of those substances will go far towards limiting misunderstanding.

It is in both a man's and a woman's best interest to discuss the situation before proceeding, even if it ruins the moment. Better to ruin the moment than the next ten years.

Reporting sexual assault

What should a woman do when she has been sexually assaulted on campus?

As soon as she is able to function at all, a woman who has been sexually assaulted should call the police, campus or local. One has the right to expect that campus police are better trained to handle such matters than city police, but, of course, that is not always the case. The police officer who responds to the call will transport the victim to a hospital, where she will be

ined for any signs of violence and given physical
to confirm recent sexual intercourse.

en if a victim is unable to report the crime
tely, she should do so later. Rape and sexual
a.   e crimes of violence. Unreported attacks
f   *Walsv* he criminal, who probably will prey on
o   *The Leader in Year* ny way this criminal can be stopped is if
the   are notified.

After the medical examination, an officer will
attempt to take the woman's statement of what happened. Many departments have women officers
assigned to the task of dealing with rape or sexual
assault victims. Some also have arrangements with victim assistance programs to have a trained counsellor
there to support a sex crime victim during this ordeal.
Taking the account of what happened is not easy for
the victim, nor for the officer. The police need a full
description of what took place, which may strike the
victim as intrusive and unsympathetic, especially right
after the crime when most victims are least able to deal
with the situation. Yet, in order to investigate, apprehend, and successfully prosecute the perpetrator, the
police must begin the investigation as early as possible.

The problem arises because our society traditionally has leered at victims of sexual offenses, rather than
viewing them in the proper light as victims of violence.
If for any reason the investigating officer misunder-
stands the nature of the offense, the victim should not
hesitate to set him straight. That is also one of the
benefits of having someone from a victim assistance
program present.

HIV testing and privacy

Can I get an anonymous HIV test?

An HIV (Human Immunodeficiency Virus) test
signals the presence in the blood stream of antigens

produced by the body to fight the HIV virus which leads to AIDS (Acquired Immunodeficiency Disease Syndrome). Currently, there is no test to determine the presence of the virus itself, so the presence of the anti-gen is the best indication.

HIV testing is recommended for anyone who has engaged in high risk behavior, which, most commonly is unprotected sexual conduct and administering drugs intravenously with a used needle or one of unknown origin. There is no such thing as *safe* sex anymore in the face of AIDS. Monogamous relationships reduce the risk, as does the use of a condom, but condoms are not fail-safe. Failure to take this precaution, however, is the equivalent of playing Russian Roulette for you and your partner. You fool yourself if you think that a con-dom is not needed because you and your partner are not engaging in "high risk" activities. AIDS has created a deadly phenomenon, so that any time you have sex with someone, you are at risk from everyone that your part-ner ever had sex with, as well as everyone with whom those people had sex.

Anonymous HIV testing is not available in every state, and many states that do have anonymous testing are limiting availability to the program or eliminating it entirely.

Anonymous testing allows a person to be tested for the presence of the virus without revealing any infor-mation about himself or herself, including identity. If anonymous testing is available in your city, your blood sample will be identified merely by a random number. You must return to the testing site to learn your test results since the clinic has no way of identifying and notifying a test taker. When you return to the clinic to learn the result, you present the technician or recep-tionist with a card you were given which has your num-ber printed on it. Use of a random number prevents anyone from knowing your HIV status unless you choose to tell that person.

Anonymous testing programs have become a volatile issue in many states. The spread of sexually transmitted diseases was traditionally monitored by health departments which collected information such as the name and address of the person stricken. This information could then be used to track the spread of the disease and to notify any partners of the risk of exposure. Some state legislatures believe that conforming HIV testing to traditional testing for other sexually transmitted diseases will help curb the rate of transmission of the HIV.

If anonymous testing is not available, is there another way to protect my identity?

Confidential testing, which is offered in every state, is the alternative to anonymous testing. It attaches your name and other identifying information (such as residence) to your test results.

Confidential testing promises to keep the results confidential among you, your health care provider, and your state health department. Your HIV status is put on record, along with your name and other identifying information, to enable the health department to observe, and hopefully manage, the transmission rate. It is the submission of this information to a government agency, obviously, that concerns some people, who worry about the security of the confidence and to what future uses the information may be put.

I understand your reluctance to share this information. However, if you have any reason to believe that you have been exposed to HIV, you should be tested. In fact, more people should be tested than think they should. Moreover, partner notification of positive test results should be undertaken immediately so that others may adjust their behavior accordingly. It is a matter both of the most common decency and of life or death.

Information about the availability of anonymous testing sites can be obtained from the federal Center for Disease Control's AIDS Hotline (1-800-432-AIDS).

6 WHAT? YOU'VE BEEN ARRESTED?

Your mother always said this would happen if you didn't change your ways! Hopefully, you are reading this, not because you have been arrested, but out of interest or in anticipation of the unlikely event that you might be someday.

There are few events in a lifetime that are more unsettling than being arrested. Most arrests are for fairly minor offenses, so few people ever anticipate being arrested. It's humiliating, frightening, and dangerous. While the humiliation can't be avoided, if you pay attention now and when it happens, you can reduce the fear and danger. It's humiliating because you've lost, hopefully for just a short period of time, immediate control over the most basic decisions; you're under the arresting officer's control. Moreover, some of the procedures to which you'll be subjected are humiliating. It's frightening because what awaits you is unknown. It's dangerous because of the people whom you will meet and the things that go on in municipal and county jails. You've seen enough television to be somewhat familiar with what happens; hopefully, I can correct some of the misinformation that you've been fed.

Arrest procedures

What exactly is an arrest?

When a police officer tells you that you're under arrest, it means that you aren't free to go, and that the officer intends to take you to the police station to file criminal charges. It's the fact that you're taken into policy custody that distinguishes an arrest from a traffic stop, where a motorist is detained briefly, while the

111

officer issues a traffic ticket and then releases the
motorist.

An arrest, however, signifies that the matter is
serious and triggers a whole different set of procedures.
Once the decision to arrest you is made, the officer will
probably handcuff you and conduct a full search of your
person. The use of handcuffs and the search are standard arrest procedure designed to protect the officer
and to prevent you from disposing of or destroying evidence of any crime which you might be carrying in your
pockets or on your body. Then the officer will place you
in the back of the police car for the ride to the police
station.

What should I expect when we get there?

You will be *booked.* Booking is an administrative
procedure, not entirely unlike registering in a new college or school. You'll be asked personal information. As
long as it's unrelated to the crime, you are obligated to
answer the questions and provide accurate information.
Some people, here and during traffic stops, think that if
they give a false name they can get off the hook. They're
wrong. It won't work, and additional charges will be
added when it's discovered that you provided false
information.

Now the similarity with school registration ends,
unless you have been to very unusual schools. You'll be
fingerprinted and photographed. If the seriousness of
what is happening has not hit you yet, fingerprinting is
sure to have that effect. Fingerprinting and photograph-
ing truly put you in the "system." They allow for computer checks to determine whether you have been in
trouble in the past under a different name; the computer will be checked at the same time under the identity you have provided. There are local, regional, state,
and national computer networks. If you have failed to
pay traffic tickets in the past, they're likely to surface,
as well as information about more serious crimes. You

are now in the system, and information about you can be retrieved in the future, unless these records are sealed or expunged.

Bail

How do I get out of here?

You are asking the right question. Don't lose sight of that goal. American jails are not safe so do whatever you can to get out of there as quickly as possible. The levels of violence and sexual assaults in jails exceed those on the most dangerous streets in the worst communities. The community holding you is responsible to see that you are safe, but chances are it won't do a very good job. The safest place is out of there. So let's focus on that.

The only justification for holding a person in jail prior to conviction is to assure that the person shows up for trial. Therefore, if the individual is from the community and not likely to run, there is really no justification for not releasing that person once he is processed. The likelihood of a person not showing up increases with the seriousness of the charge and the harshness of potential punishment. Thus, the more serious the charge, the higher the bail or the more stringent the alternative or additional conditions of release. Traditionally, pretrial release is unavailable to persons charged with murder because no matter how much bail is required, the person may run to avoid facing the possible penalty.

Some people are simply so dangerous that releasing them back into the community almost assures that other crimes will be committed and other people hurt. In that instance, it has been determined that a person may be held in jail until trial. Recognizing that it's very difficult to predict future behavior accurately, pretrial detention should be reserved for those situations where the arrestee has a history of committing violent crimes, and the proof of the current charge is substantial.

Will they hold me even if I'm charged with a less serious crime?

Most people arrested are charged with relatively minor offenses—misdemeanors. Although not minor to the person facing the charge or to the person harmed by the conduct, such offenses are minor in comparison to felonies. A misdemeanor generally carries a maximum sentence in a local jail, not a state prison, of less than one year, and most people convicted of misdemeanors are not sentenced to any jail time at all. A person charged with a misdemeanor who lives in the community will usually show up in court as required, rather than become a fugitive. The law takes account of that likelihood.

If you're arrested for a misdemeanor, chances are you'll be released after you're booked. Most communities allow for "jailhouse" or "station house" bail for misdemeanors. There is no reason to introduce you into the jailhouse population, with all of its problems and dangers, when the charge is relatively minor, like a misdemeanor, and you have a local address. It is in the community's interest, as well as your own to keep you out of the jail. The more people jailed, the greater the security problem and the greater the cost. Fortunately yours and the community's interests coincide.

If bail were to be set by a judge, you would have to wait at least until the following morning or over a weekend until court is in session. (Sorry, few communities have night courts.) To avoid jailing you until a judge appears to set bail, the court has provided the police or sheriff with a bail schedule for minor offenses, detailing how much money to require in return for your release. The money put up for bail is returnable when you show up for trial.

Where cash bail is required, you may have to wait a while until friends or family show up with the requisite amount. You may be lucky enough to be in a community where your signature on a statement promising to appear in court is enough to gain instant release. This is known as release on your own recognizance. However, if you've been arrested for drunk driving, common sense dictates that the police hold you until you're sober and able to drive home, or until someone comes for you.

What if I'm charged with a felony?

Those charged with more serious crimes—felonies—will not be released from the jail until a judge evaluates the case and sets bail; consequently, there will be a wait in jail until court is in session. The arraignment to set bail should take place within forty-eight hours, unless a week-end intervenes. Anyway, the bail set will be higher than for a misdemeanor, and the money probably could not be raised as quickly as the lesser sum required for misdemeanors. So a period in jail is inevitable except in those few cities where people arrested are taken directly to courts which run throughout the day and night. The higher that bail is set, the more likely it is that you will need a bail bondsman. A bondsman secures an arrestee's release by promising to pay the court the full amount of the bond if the arrestee fails to appear for trial. The bondsman does this for a fee, usually ten percent of the face value of the bond, and only if the arrestee or a relative or friend can turn over to the bondsman a deed to property or bank books equal to the face value of the bond.

One phone call

When do I get my phone call?

Under our legal system, you are presumed innocent until proven guilty. And some people charged with crimes actually are, in fact, innocent. To live up to that, our society tries to prevent incommunicado incarceration. In other words, society doesn't want you being locked away without anyone knowing what has happened to you. James Madison, the author of the Bill of Rights, didn't have a telephone, but allowing a person arrested access to a telephone is consistent with the rights Madison did include in the Bill of Rights. You have the right to let someone know where you are and what your situation is so that efforts can be initiated to get you out.

Your access to a telephone is guaranteed by law in most states. It should not be "a phone call" as you put it. What if the line is busy? Or no one is home? You should have the opportunity to place calls until you reach someone who can act on your information.

Choose carefully whom you call and notify of your predicament. Make sure that the person is dependable and will be willing to help you out. If your immediate family is in the vicinity, calling them would be a wise first choice. They are the ones you are likely to look to for bail money, if needed, and to help you get an attorney.

When your family isn't nearby, you have to make a choice. It might be advisable to contact someone who is in the vicinity, and ask that person to coordinate your efforts by contacting family and trying to get bail money from them. On the other hand, it might be easier to deal directly with your family, although since they are far away, they are in no position to handle matters locally except to contact an attorney. Even if your family is far away, though, they might be the ones to contact, if they aren't likely to fall apart, and are able to mobilize someone locally who can help you. Otherwise, their input will be to send money, and you'll still have to find someone locally who will quarterback activities until you are released and able to do things for yourself.

Having to call around until you find someone willing to take on the responsibility can add to your anxiety. Call your family; they are less likely to ignore your cry for help.

Miranda rights

Hey, no one read me my rights!

You've been watching too much television again! The rights you're referring to are *Miranda* rights (named after the U.S. Supreme Court case, *Miranda vs. Arizona*, which stated them). These rights must be read to you only prior to questioning. Some police departments require that the rights be read to everyone who is arrested; however, that is local policy and isn't required by the Constitution. If police don't intend to question you, they need not advise you of these rights. Nor do they have to stop you from blurting out a statement while they advise you of the rights. *Miranda* protection only kicks in if the police wish to interrogate you after you're in custody, not if you make a statement which isn't in response to questioning or before you're actually in custody. Most people charged with misdemeanors are never questioned and, therefore, may never be read *Miranda* rights.

What exactly are *Miranda* rights?

Assuming that you're to be questioned, *Miranda* rights are helpful *but not a cure-all.* So pay attention! The rules have become very technical. I'll tell you here what you *need* to know to protect your rights and to keep from harming yourself.

In case you've never watched television, you need to know that the police officer, *prior* to interrogation, must tell you the following: YOU HAVE THE RIGHT TO REMAIN SILENT. ANYTHING YOU SAY CAN AND WILL BE USED AGAINST YOU IN A COURT OF LAW. YOU HAVE THE RIGHT TO AN ATTOR-

NEY. IF YOU CANNOT AFFORD AN ATTORNEY,
ONE WILL BE APPOINTED FOR YOU.

The officer just told you that *anything* you say to
the police officer may come back to haunt you later in a
criminal trial. Since he also told you that you don't
have to say anything, why would you? Further, you
have the right to have a lawyer guide you through this
thicket, and the state is obligated to furnish you with a
lawyer if you can't afford one.

After the officer informs you of these rights, he'll
ask you if you are willing to waive them and talk with
him about the crime for which you've been arrested. At
any time, the interrogators may switch and ask you
questions about one or more different crimes. The
questioning is not limited to the crimes for which
you've been arrested, and you needn't be told in
advance that they will question you about other crimes.
If you waive your rights at the outset, the interrogator
doesn't have to get a new waiver to question you about
a different crime. It isn't unusual for police interrogators to sneak in questions about other crimes, nor is
it unusual for these *other* crimes to be the primary
purpose for the interrogation. In other words, despite
Miranda it is still a cat-and-mouse game. Make no
mistake about it: *you are the mouse.*

Remaining silent

**But still you're saying that it is entirely up to me whether I
want to answer any questions?**

Exactly. Since it is your choice whether to waive
your rights and talk to the officer, ultimately you are
the one in control. Even if you initially consent, you can
stop the questioning at any time by saying so or by
requesting a lawyer. The officer must heed your request
to stop questioning, and, if you request a lawyer, may
not question you without one present. Note, however,
that, although police will usually seek a written waiver,

because it is better evidence that you actually did consent to questioning, a written waiver is not strictly required, and an oral waiver can be valid. It is up to the police to show that you waived your rights or made statements voluntarily, in order for the statements to be used against you in a criminal trial.

A valid waiver of your *Miranda* rights goes a long way towards showing that your statements were made voluntarily. If, however, the waiver, or the statements themselves, were obtained through the use of coercion or unreasonable intimidation which overcomes your ability to exercise your free will, then the statements were not voluntary, with or without a *Miranda* waiver, and cannot be used against you. Coercion can be express or implied, physical or psychological, and may include such things as the police questioning you for an extended period of time; denying you basic necessities during questioning, such as food, water, or the use of a restroom; threatening you, your friends, or your family if you don't answer questions; or making unfulfillable promises of leniency or assistance if you "cooperate." Since obtaining a "confession" makes the officers' job much easier, some may not hesitate to use the more subtle methods of coercion.

When is it in my best interest to waive these rights and answer their questions?

Never! On any given day on the planet there may be a few situations where it would be in a suspect's best interests to cooperate with the police, but those situations are so specialized that they won't apply to 99% of the people arrested and questioned. Count on the fact that you aren't one of the exceptions. You cannot talk your way out of trouble. In fact, you're much more likely to complicate your situation than to make it better. When the officer advised you that *"anything* you say can and will be used against you," he was not misleading you. Some people think that so long as they don't incriminate themselves for the crime charged they aren't hurting themselves. Wrong!

First, I've already told you that the crime charged may not be the one the police most want to question you about. Second, even though you may think you're helping yourself, if, for instance, you present the police with an alibi, any untruth or even discrepancy in your story may come back later to plague you at trial. Thus, it's probably not in your best interest to share with the police, at this time, even information tending to show your innocence, without the assistance of a lawyer. If you have an alibi defense, let your lawyer develop it and unfold it for the police and prosecutor at the appropriate time. Don't try to save on lawyer's fees here. It's too crucial and you don't know what you're doing!

Keep in mind, you don't have to prove your innocence. The state has to prove your guilt. Moreover, as I said, it's very unlikely that you can talk yourself out of trouble. When a police officer suggests you do talk yourself out of trouble, remember, he is there to help convict you.

Understood. But won't the police officers dislike me if I refuse to answer any questions?

Good point. It doesn't matter whether the police officers like you or not. If they think you have committed a crime, and suggest they will like you if you tell them all about it, they're only sweet-talking you into implicating yourself. Telling you they have nothing against you is only an act to disarm you and get you to cooperate. On the other hand, there is no reason why they should treat you disrespectfully, either. All of this should be handled professionally and impersonally.

Got it. Should I tell them I don't want to talk with them?

You could, but you can protect yourself better if you tell them you want a lawyer. Sometimes knowing a little legal mumbo jumbo can come in handy, and this is one of those times. There will be a significant difference in how the police act, depending entirely on how you tell them you don't want to talk with them or answer their questions. This shouldn't be so, but legally those differences turn on what words you use.

You place yourself in the strongest position if you say, "I do not want to talk with you without a lawyer," or even just, "I want a lawyer." Then don't say anything else until you've seen a lawyer and have instructions from the lawyer. By telling the police that you want a lawyer, your statement is interpreted to mean that you don't feel able to deal with them except with the assistance of a lawyer's help. As a result, the police may not question you about the initial charges or *any* crime, without a lawyer present to assist you.

It is important that you don't say anything after asking for a lawyer that the police could interpret as your consent to start discussing the crime again. If you initiate questioning or a dialogue with the police on your own, any resulting statements may be used against you. Even the innocuous comment, "What is going to happen now?" was interpreted by the U.S. Supreme Court as initiating discussion about the crime, even though the suspect may have been asking about where they were going to put him, when they were going to feed him, or when he would have access to a bathroom. The best advice I can give you is: tell the police you want a lawyer and then tell them nothing more.

The problem with exercising your right to silence ("I don't want to talk to you" or "I don't want to answer your questions"), rather than your right to counsel, is that the police may come back at you after an interval and try again. If, instead, you tell them you want a lawyer, they cannot come back at you again until you have seen a lawyer, *and* you have the right to have that lawyer with you if there are any future attempts to interrogate you. The differences are real and vast and turn on which words you use.

Getting a lawyer

How am I supposed to know which lawyer to pick?

If you're in trouble, choosing a lawyer is one of the most important things you have to do. You'll pay a lawyer to see you through this crisis, and to make sure that it comes out as well as possible under the circumstances.

When you're not in jail and need to select a lawyer, don't hesitate to shop around. Lawyers' fees differ drastically. A lawyer may charge you by the hour or may have a predetermined fee for the particular service which you seek. Don't make your selection based only on cost, but it is a factor to consider. If a lawyer's fee differs radically from several others whom you have consulted, there may well be a reason, in terms of quality of service, experience, and results, for the difference in fees. If so, the savings wouldn't be worth the ultimate cost. On the other hand, one lawyer's fee may be much higher than another's because of reputation and demand created more by advertising and public relations, than by ability and performance.

So how can you know which lawyer to hire? The best way to pick a lawyer is to check with friends and relatives who have used lawyers and ask their opinions. If a friend recommends a lawyer whom she has used, it is fairly certain that your friend was satisfied with the lawyer. Check with others as to that lawyer's reputation. Interview a few lawyers. Listen carefully to what they say and how they react to your situation, and evaluate their familiarity with your particular kind of problem.

A lawyer need not know everything about every subject; lawyers can research the law and handle new problems. That is what they are taught in law school—how to approach new and different problems. However, familiarity is helpful. You would not want a lawyer to handle your criminal trial if she only writes wills and never goes to court. In the same vein, if you are looking for a will or want to set up a business, you would do better with a lawyer who practices in those areas rather than one who specializes in criminal defense work. Most importantly, after your interviews, try to determine which lawyer put you most at ease and made you feel the most confident.

It's important to distinguish between false confidence and real competence so heed the following advice. Dismiss the lawyer who assures you that he or she can produce a specific result. Be prepared to distinguish between the lawyer who guarantees a result, and the lawyer who tells you that in most cases like yours a particular result is likely, if certain conditions exist. The one who claims to guarantee a result is just trying to snow you; it is a guarantee that will be forgotten very quickly. The other lawyer is not offering a guarantee she cannot keep, but is demonstrating familiarity with the subject matter and court.

But if I'm in jail and can't go round to different lawyers' offices, how do I know which one to hire?

If you are in jail, you do not have the luxury to shop around as suggested. Here you are more dependent on recommendations of friends and relatives. You need a lawyer who will respond quickly to your call for help. But don't panic. Your choice of a lawyer can be provisional. Moreover, the police won't start an interrogation without you, and your lawyer is not likely to consent to your being interrogated anyway. You can use the lawyer you get to merely advise you on what to do while you're in jail and to help you get bailed out. If you aren't comfortable with the attorney who responded to your call for help, you are free, after paying that lawyer for the time spent on your case, to interview several lawyers and decide whom you want to represent you the rest of the way.

One word of caution in choosing a lawyer: Beware of lawyers recommended by jailers. While they will represent you as zealously as other lawyers, they are probably recommended by a jailer because he gets a fee if you act on his recommendation. A jailer's praise for a particular lawyer may be based more on the prospective fee, than on the lawyer's past accomplishments.

Should I wait for the lawyer to call me about my case's progress or to bring up the question of fees, or should I initiate such discussions?

You have the right to expect your lawyer to keep on top of your case and to communicate often with you. If, though, you call every day with questions about details, a lawyer will tire of you quickly. However, if you do not bother the lawyer unnecessarily, you have the right to expect her to take your calls or return them promptly, and to keep you informed of what is happening in your case. At the outset tell the lawyer you select of your expectations.

The lawyer should freely discuss her fee with you and explain what it covers. The lawyer should tell you whether a requested amount of money covers the entire case or just the preliminaries, and whether you will be asked for more money as the case proceeds through court. In a criminal case, a lawyer's fee will vary depending on whether the case goes to trial or a plea of guilty is entered. All of this is information which will help you make an intelligent decision whom to hire. If anything isn't explained clearly to you, by all means ask for specifics.

Unless time is absolutely of the essence, such as if you are due in court the following day, do not make your decision in one lawyer's office. You are probably making a decision based solely on your reaction to the lawyer's personality, if you make the decision on the spot. Take an evening to evaluate the lawyers with whom you met. Try to find additional opinions about the lawyers' skills, integrity, and attention to their clients' inquiries, and then make your decision.

I don't have any money to hire a lawyer. How will I get my attorney?

The *Miranda* rights you were read specifically included a statement assuring you that, if you are without funds to hire an attorney, one will be provided for you. Attorneys are provided in several different ways to handle advising suspects prior to and during interrogation. A contract lawyer provided by Legal Aid or the Public Defender's office may be called in to advise you at this point, or a court will appoint an attorney for you. You usually won't have a say in choosing your lawyer, but the same standard of competency that is applicable to retained or hired lawyers also applies to appointed lawyers.

When a police officer tells you that a court will appoint an attorney to represent you, ordinarily it means that you will not see an attorney until after you appear in court. Do not panic. While it is helpful and comforting to see an attorney immediately, if you do not lose your head, you will not be hurt by the delay. Remember, if you request an attorney, the police may not attempt to interrogate you until after you have seen a lawyer, nor without the lawyer being present during interrogation. By all means, don't become talkative out of disappointment or increased anxiety resulting from not having immediate access to an attorney. That could have disastrous effects and will be portrayed as your decision to discuss the case without an attorney. Control your anxiety and remain silent.

Going to jail

Are they going to put me in jail?

If you have not been released on bail or on your own promise to appear in court, you will be placed in a jail cell until it is time for your court appearance. You may be placed in a large cell, where prisoners waiting to see a judge are kept away from the general inmate population, or you may be integrated into the jail population and placed in a smaller cell to await your court appearance. Prior to being integrated into the jail population, you may be strip-searched to make sure that you are not hiding a weapon or drugs anywhere on your body. It is part of the degrading experience of being in jail.

Can I talk to the people in my jail cell?

If you were out on the street, you would not walk up to absolute strangers and confide personal information in them. Why would you do so in a jail, where there is every likelihood that the people you meet are, on average, less reliable than strangers met on the street? Misery loves company, but that company may not be worth the cost.

Prisoners frequently report what is told to them by cellmates to the jailers, who pass it on for use at trial. They make these reports in hopes of getting favorable treatment in their own cases. Often, cellmates are promised in advance some consideration for passing on helpful information. If you confide in your cellmate, you may later be very disappointed to find that cellmate testifying about what you said at your trial. If you are involved in a major investigation, that cellmate could even be a police officer planted in the cell to come up with information.

Resist the temptation, as well as the exhortations of your cellmates, to confide in them. Don't admit to the crime. Better yet, avoid all discussion about the charges. Your cellmates can't help you; they can only hurt you.

Don't panic!

For the last time, when am I getting out of here?

If for some reason you were not eligible for jailhouse bail, could not raise the bail required by the schedule, or have been charged with a crime where bail must be set by the judge, don't panic. You will have another opportunity to secure your release when you appear in court. Make sure at that time that the attorney who is present to assist all prisoners knows that you do not have the money to post bond. Ask the attorney to inquire about release without cash bail for you.

If there is no attorney at the initial hearing, one will be appointed shortly thereafter, but advise the judge, when you are in front of the bench, of your inability to make bail. Politely, provide the judge with information about your ties to the community—how long you have lived there, whether you have family there, and whether you have steady employment—and then ask for "personal release." This is release that is not secured by a bail bond but is either just a promise to appear or a promise to pay an amount of money if you do not appear (which will be collected when you are apprehended). You have nothing to lose by asking, and it just might gain you your freedom. In any event, as soon as you have a lawyer, the request may be renewed.

Unfortunately, some people never gain their freedom while awaiting trial. That is more true of persons charged with serious offenses, felonies, but it can be true also of people charged with misdemeanors.

Well, what's going to happen now?

You don't need me anymore. Whether you are free on bail or still in jail, your lawyer will guide you the rest of the way. With your lawyer's advice and assistance, you will decide whether it is in your best interest to plead guilty to the charge or a lesser offense (if the prosecutor is willing to reduce the charge), or whether to plead not guilty and go to trial.

From here on, your lawyer will be at your side every step of the way. Your lawyer will help you prepare to answer the court's questions if you plead guilty or what to say if you go to trial and testify. Your lawyer will even help you plan how to dress. Take your lawyer's advice seriously. If you don't understand that advice, or if you disagree with it, tell your lawyer and discuss it with him. Not understanding what your lawyer says doesn't make you dumb, but remaining silent, when you don't understand, does.

GOOD LUCK!

7 ON TAXES

Although not an overriding concern, students and young people, in general, do face some tax problems.

Unfortunately, few of us think about taxes until around April 15. If we haven't planned ahead, we might be unpleasantly surprised at that time by how much we owe. Planning is unlikely to reduce the amount owed, but it can make the payment less painful.

I am a full-time student, and my parents claim me as a dependent. I earn about $2200 a year at a part-time job and in the summer. I thought my earnings were tax free, however, when I got my paycheck money had been taken out.

A student who counts on a certain amount of money from summer and part-time employment makes several assumptions about forthcoming paychecks. Those assumptions may be wrong, leading to serious shortfalls in expected savings for school.

Often, a student assumes that his paycheck will be exempt from taxes if the student doesn't earn a great deal and remains a dependent of his parents. All too often forgotten in these calculations are the other taxes which are deducted from paychecks, and which may reduce take-home pay below the expected amount.

Full-time students who are claimed as dependents by their parents may earn up to $3400 without paying federal income tax on those earnings. However, there are other deductions from your payroll check besides federal income tax. Social Security and Medicare payroll taxes are 7.65%, and are deducted regardless of whether you owe federal income tax. Additionally, state and local income taxes may be deducted from your paycheck, accounting for your reduced take-home pay. If money was withheld for federal income taxes, you will be eligible for a refund.

I'm in the same situation and understand the deductions from my paycheck. I also earned $2200 over the summer and received about $300 in interest on a savings account. What I don't understand is why I owed federal income tax when I filed my return last year.

The exemption from federal income tax, of up to $3400, applies only to salary and wage income. It does not apply to interest or dividend income. When the exemption is figured, it will be based only on salary and wages. Any salary or wages above $3400 *and* any interest or dividend income is taxable. In your situation, you owed no taxes on your earnings because they were under $3400, but you did owe federal income tax on your interest income. You would pay that amount when you file your federal income tax return, after receipt of your W-2 form. If federal income tax was withheld from your wages, the amount of tax owed on your savings account interest will be deducted from your refund.

My wife and I both work, and taxes are withheld from both of our paychecks. Unfortunately, the amount withheld never seems to be enough, and each year we end up owing more federal and state taxes. What should we do?

First, check to make sure that neither you nor your wife has claimed an exemption *and* a dependent. In a perfect system, you should each take one exemption, and the amounts should work out. But, it does rot always work out perfectly. It may be that your combined incomes push you into the next higher tax bracket, and each of you were withheld at the lower tax rate, thus accounting for your owing taxes.

There are ways to remedy the situation. However, each involves increasing the amount withheld, resulting in a combined lower take home pay. One of you can claim no exemptions and the other one exemption. If the shortfall in the amount withheld is not great, that should solve the problem by increasing the amount withheld from one paycheck. An alternative is to request your employer to deduct an additional amount of taxes each week or month to make up the shortfall. Naturally, if you increase the amount withheld above the amount owed, you will be entitled to a refund when you file your tax return.

There is another possibility, which you might consider, that would decrease your overall tax liability. Instead of filing joint tax returns, as most husbands and wives do, figure out whether you would be paying less taxes if you filed separate returns. In some cases, there is a slight increase in the amount paid to the federal government, but a larger savings in the amount paid to the state government, resulting in an overall reduction in the amount of taxes paid. Don't be hesitant to try the various combinations. You might be surprised at the amount saved.

My withholding was reduced, and I have a second job at which I am withheld at a low tax rate. I know that I am going to owe a lot of money which I do not have. Can I wait to file until I have the money?

No. File your tax return on time *even if you do not have the money to pay what you owe.* The Internal Revenue Service will work out a payment schedule, but it is up to you to make this request before the filing deadline. You are required to file your income tax return by April 15. Failure to do so or to pay taxes owed can result in your owing interest and penalties or in criminal prosecution. You can get an extension which allows you a three-month delay on the filing deadline, but all taxes owed must be paid prior to or along with the request for an extension.

I have a partial scholarship. Is it tax free?

Scholarships and fellowships awarded to degree candidates are not taxable. The amount may include fees, books, and supplies required for particular courses. Athletic scholarships are not taxable, even though student athletes are expected to participate in sports.

There are, however, many other forms of educational assistance, and not all are treated the same. Where an employer pays an employee's educational expenses, up to $5,250 per year of the amount received is not included in the employee's income and, thus, is tax free. Any sum above that amount is included in the employee's gross income and is subject to income tax withholding.

Employees of educational institutions and their dependents often receive tuition reductions. Tuition reductions below the graduate or professional school levels are not taxable. Tuition reductions for graduate and professional school are taxable, and the institution is required to include the amount in the employee's gross income that is subject to income tax withholding. Graduate tuition grants, though, for graduate teaching and research assistants are not taxable. Amounts paid, in addition to tuition reductions, to graduate assistants for teaching and research services are taxable.

8 ABOUT CREDIT

Credit is one of those commodities you can have all you want when you don't need it, but probably can't get when you really do. Today, many college students and young people in the work force need credit, and all will find it useful. For many of you, the loan process, student, car, or otherwise, is your first experience with credit. Your younger years provide you with the opportunity to develop a credit history that will be available when you get out of school or start a family. It is also a time when you can develop a bad credit rating which will haunt you for years.

The mass use of credit cards extends only over the past thirty years. If you ask your grandparents, they will probably tell you that they had no credit cards before 1960. The credit cards that did exist before then were issued only by department stores to their regular, best customers. The first mass credit cards were issued by oil companies, and were an attempt to build customer loyalty. Rather than shop around for the cheapest gasoline, consumers became dependent on the card, and were likely to pay a penny or two more for the familiar brand. While you are probably being inundated by offers of credit cards, the earliest credit cards were difficult to obtain. People who were denied credit had no recourse in those days. Fortunately, that has changed.

Should I have credit cards?

While young or in school, you should begin developing a positive credit history. Many companies and banks will offer you credit cards. Once you have a credit card and do not default on the payments, subsequent cards will be easy to obtain.

Some credit cards being offered to you, as a student or young person with no credit history, require a guarantor, usually a parent, who agrees to guarantee payment if you default on the obligation. These initial offers carry a small credit line, $300 to $500, which allows the holder to charge up to that amount. As you use your card, the merchant will seek authorization from the credit card company for the amount of the purchase. Visa, Mastercard, or one of the others, will put a hold on your account for the amount of the purchase. When those holds add up to your credit limit, additional purchase authorizations will be refused. You are then billed at some time during the month for the balance. If you pay the full amount, then the full line of credit will be restored. If you make a partial payment, your credit line will be restored up to the amount of the payment, and new charges will be authorized.

The key, while you are young, single, or in school, is to have a credit card which you use as infrequently as possible. Don't even carry it with you. If you can't pay for an item out of present earnings or savings, chances are you shouldn't buy it.

Put the card away for an emergency or to pay for a trip home. If you are fortunate and there are no emergencies, use it once or twice a year to establish a credit history. Pay it off immediately. And don't carry a balance.

How should I select a credit card?

Good question. Credit cards are not all the same, even though they may carry the same Visa or Mastercard logos. All Visa and Master cards may look alike, but their terms may differ drastically. Those terms are set by the bank or other institution that issues the card. You have to shop around and compare the terms being offered by the credit card issuer to determine which card will cost you the least.

The credit card companies make money in several ways. Before selecting Visa or Mastercard, check to see how many ways, and how much the issuing bank will charge you.

For example, many banks charge an annual fee for their Visa or Mastercard. Not all banks charge the annual fee, and, among those that do, the fee varies. You should be able to shop around and find a card that does not charge an annual fee. Many newspapers run weekly lists of the best credit card deals in the area.

The merchants selling you goods and services on credit are charged a percentage of your purchase price for the convenience of having the credit card company bill you and collect the money owed. However, the bank may try to collect twice by charging you interest from the date of the purchase. When interest is charged from the date of purchase, you will pay interest on the money spent up until the date payment is received, even if you pay off the total balance when billed.

Other banks charge the card holder no interest on purchases, if the card holder pays the full amount owed each month and does not carry a balance. Obviously, it costs you less to charge, if your card is issued by a bank that gives the card holder a grace period, and charges no interest unless there is a balance which is not paid off by the due date. The Discover card pays you a very minimal amount at the end of the year, determined by the total that you charged against the card during the year. The amount is negligible, but not insignificant, when compared to some cards which charge you interest on each purchase, from the date of the purchase.

If you carry a balance, you will be charged interest every month. Department stores and oil companies charge you interest every month, as well, on the unpaid balance of your bill. It stands to reason, then, that you should pay off your credit cards as quickly as possible. Every time you pay interest on a past purchase, you have increased the cost of that item or service.

When you are selecting a credit card, read the terms and conditions which are included along with the application. Aim for a card that: (1) charges no annual fee; (2) offers you a grace period on purchases so that if you pay off your bill each month you are not charged interest; and (3) charges the lowest annual interest rate. If you don't understand the written explanation, don't be bashful. Call the bank's 800-number and find out the answers to the above three questions. If they don't have an 800-number, forget them and choose a different bank.

What are the major pitfalls to watch out for?

Obviously, the major problem is overspending. By charging purchases to your card in an amount more than you currently have, you are committing future funds which you are not sure you will have when the bill comes. Even if you can pay off these purchases over the succeeding six months, keep in mind that you are limiting your ability to purchase other items during that period, as well as running up interest. Since your credit record applies to all transactions, if you overextend on your credit cards and cannot pay them, you will adversely affect your ability to get loans.

The more you use the card, the more the credit card company stands to make. Obviously, then, their advertisements are intended to get you to use their card and to spend, spend, spend. Don't, don't, don't.

Everyday we see a great many items in stores, in ads, or on commercials for items we might like to have. Some we need; most we don't, but we'd take them if they were offered for free. One of the psychological tools used to sell goods or services in our society is to make us believe that these goods or services are free or virtually without cost. A great many people suffer from the mind set that if they do not have to pay for them at the moment, the goods or services are, in fact, free. Thus, they end up using the card too often for impulse or frivolous purchases. Eventually, the bill will come and will have to be paid.

A common source of problems is the student or young person who sees an item that he wants and decides to charge it, intending to pay for it when next month's allowance or paycheck arrives. By that time, the car may need repair, you may need to see a dentist, or other items or services may be offered which you really need or would rather have than the previous month's purchases. The problem is that the money coming in has already been committed to the past charges. A vicious cycle develops because the undisciplined consumer can't just turn off the "wants," even though all immediate and future money has been committed to these past purchases. Unless the consumer puts the cards away and stops buying until past purchases are paid off, a perpetual cycle of debt lies ahead.

If you meet minimum monthly payments, but have extended your credit to the limit, the bank may increase your credit limit. By allowing you to charge more, the bank stands to profit more. It's not doing you a favor. If you are barely meeting monthly payments without making a dent in the outstanding balance, you already are overextended. Most of your monthly payment is going for interest, and you have yet to start paying off the purchases. You can't afford any more credit; don't be misled by the bank's generosity. At the rate you are going, you may still be paying off this year's purchases three years from now.

The interest charged on the balance is often outrageous. Banks that are presently paying three percent interest to depositors are charging anywhere from 8 (and they're the best, except for special banking customers!), 12, 16 or even 20 percent on credit card balances. Figure that out for yourself. The bank is paying a customer three percent to let the bank use the customer's money, and then turns around and charges double digit interest. Neat profit, isn't it? Even if you don't begrudge the bank that excess profit, try to figure out how expensive each of your purchases has become. If it takes you a year to pay off a sweater that you just had to have because it was on sale, and you are paying 19% interest, that sweater is no longer a bargain.

Even if you pay off your credit bill balance each month, always have an idea during the month of how much you have charged. That way, you will know how much of your monthly budget must go towards the credit card bill that month. That knowledge will help you to restrain yourself. Don't rely on the credit card company to cut you off. If they authorize over your set limit, you still have to pay.

My loan application was turned down because of poor credit. What can I do?

If you are denied credit for a loan, there is an appeal process. Where a denial of credit is based on a *credit report*, the lending institution is required to notify the applicant which *credit reporting agency* provided the adverse credit report. By law, you are entitled to a free copy of the credit report from the reporting agency if your request is received within 60 days of the denial. After 60 days, you have to pay for the report.

Once you get the report, you will learn who provided the adverse information about your credit. That information provides you with the opportunity to go directly to that company or bank, and to either clear up the error or pay the unpaid bill, straightening out your credit rating. This does not necessarily mean that you must pay the full bill immediately. The lender will want you to clear up the bill to its standard, which, under federal law, may not be an unreasonable standard.

Maybe you don't owe anything to the company; maybe you never even had an account with that company. Errors in credit files are not unusual, simply because of the sheer numbers of files and entries involved. It is amazing that there are not more errors than there are. When contacting the source of the negative credit information, ask the customer representative to check your account under the account number listed on the credit report. Is the name the same? It is not uncommon for people to have the same names. Ask them to check the address on the account and the social security number, as well. Often, errors of this nature can be corrected quickly and over the phone. If the store or bank wants you to send a copy of the credit reporting agency's report, rather than dealing with it then and there over the phone, ask why the matter cannot be handled on the phone. If you do not get a satisfactory answer, ask to speak with a supervisor. It is in your interest to resolve this matter as quickly as possible.

Once you and the source of the poor credit information have discovered the error or resolved the outstanding bill, make sure that you get a letter from them to that effect. *You* should then send a copy of the correction letter to the credit reporting agency. Find out from that agency what other reporting agencies may be carrying a file on you. Then obtain reports from these agencies, so that errors, if any, can be corrected. Remember to keep copies of all correspondence. Do not rely on the source of the original information to send the letter directly to the credit reporting agency. There are too many computers talking to each other and too many opportunities for slip ups; you want control so that you can be sure that the proper papers are transmitted.

If I'm not presently applying for credit, how do I check my current credit rating to find out if I'm in trouble?

It's a good idea not to wait for credit problems to check your credit. You may request a credit report from any credit reporting agency operating in your area. TRW, one of the largest credit reporting agencies in the country, offers a free credit report once a year to each person, in addition to the credit reports which they are obligated to furnish free following a denial of credit.

In order to get your free credit report, you must provide them with the following information: (1) name (last, first and middle initial, as well as any designations such as junior or senior); (2) spouse's name, if you are married; (3) your present address and zip code, and any other addresses you have had during the previous five years; (4) your social security number; and (5) your year of birth. Send that information, along with a copy of your driver's license or a current bill with your address on it, for verification purposes, to the following address:

TRW Complimentary Report Request
P.O. Box 2350
Chattsworth, California 91313-2350.

Take advantage of this free offer to make sure that your credit rating is okay, and that there are no errors in your credit file. TRW is not providing these reports free of charge purely out of charity. There was enough controversy surrounding erroneous information contained in these credit reports that TRW, for public relations purposes and to avoid liability, decided to provide the public with periodic free access to this information for verification purposes. Now is a good time to check; don't wait until you have been denied credit.

9   ON THE JOB

Many of the issues we've already discussed also come up in the employment context. Specifically, an employee's right to be treated fairly, not to be discriminated against, and not to be fired arbitrarily are the issues which we'll talk about here. Almost a hundred years ago, American workers had very few rights. Those rights were expanded during the course of this century, but have been threatened again because of the weakening of unions, the failing economy and the scarcity of jobs, and the greater reluctance of government to interfere and regulate employers.

I have an interview for a job that I want very much. Do I have to disclose a drunk driving conviction which was removed or expunged from my record?

How much negative information to divulge on a job application is always a tough question. Naturally, the prospective employer wants truthful and full answers. Frequently, those answers will be used to disqualify an applicant, even though the applicant may be able to give a perfectly valid explanation, if given an opportunity. Obviously, the bottom line answer is to disclose as little adverse information as possible. You have to walk a fine line, however, providing enough information so as not to get caught in a trap if the employer checks on your answers, yet not volunteering too much information which could result in your immediate disqualification.

In your situation, if you are asked on the application whether you have ever been convicted of a crime, you need not answer affirmatively. The state where you were convicted provided a procedure to remove the record of that conviction, if you satisfied certain conditions: generally speaking if at the end of one year you have had no other convictions, your record is cleared. If you have satisfied the state that no record of your prior offense needs to be maintained, your prospective employer has no right to this information and is not going to be able to find it. On the other hand, if the question is whether you have ever been arrested, you should be advised that expungement of a conviction does not also result in the sealing of arrest records. That information should not be readily accessible, but often is. When the prior conviction is a juvenile offense, you are under no obligation to disclose that information.

Sometimes it makes sense to provide every possible bit of information. Your honesty, in those situations, may offset any negative impact caused by the (hopefully isolated) youthful indiscretion or temporary lapse of judgment. For example, anytime you apply for a state license, or apply to take a bar examination, you should err on the side of disclosure. Each form will provide you with the opportunity to explain any arrests or convictions. If the form does not provide space for an explanation, attach a separate sheet. While a record of a prior arrest or conviction may not prevent you from being licensed, the failure to disclose that information may be sufficient to cause revocation of your license at a later time, if the information surfaces.

My employer recently announced periodic, random drug testing. Do I have to submit?

Only if you want to keep your job. Drug testing has become very common in the workplace in the last decade. This is just another example of how we have come to accept losses of privacy in our society. There are certain restrictions, however. Your employer may not require drug testing if it is prohibited by statute in your state, if your job is governed by a collective bargaining agreement which affects your employer and bars drug testing, or, possibly, if you work for the government. Otherwise, drug testing may be required by your employer as a precondition to employment and a condition of continued employment.

Government employees enjoy greater protection, but are not immune from drug testing. Drug testing constitutes a search and must meet the reasonableness standards of the Fourth Amendment. The Fourth Amendment protection applies only to searches by governmental entities, and therefore does not protect against searches by private employers.

Ordinarily, government employees may be subjected to drug testing only if there is reason to suspect that the employee to be tested is a drug abuser. Random drug testing without individualized suspicion is only permissible in certain ultrasensitive jobs, such as for prison guards and those involved in the enforcement of the drug laws. In positions like these, the government has a compelling interest to ensure that drug policies are not being violated. A governmental entity could probably make a successful argument in favor of random drug testing for any employee involved in law enforcement, at least those who carry firearms. For other government employees in less sensitive positions, the argument in favor of random drug testing is not as strong, and the Fourth Amendment will probably prohibit drug testing without individualized suspicion.

I work for the post office, where department regulations claim the right to look through employee lockers at any time and for any reason. Is there anything that I can do about this?

The same policies which apply to drug testing apply to searches of an employee's locker, office, or possessions by a supervisor. If you were employed in the private sector, you would have no recourse against your employer's policy to inspect employee lockers and possessions, except, perhaps, through your union, which might raise the issue in negotiations or a job action. The weakened position of labor unions, of course, limits the union's clout on these issues and may result in the union's conserving its influence for economic issues.

You, however, indicate that you work in the post office, and thus you have broader rights than an employee in the private sector. Again, as in drug testing, the governmental entity's authority to conduct searches of its employees must meet the Fourth Amendment reasonableness standard. An employee has a lesser expectation of privacy on the job than he would have at home. Even though it is a lesser expectation of privacy, it is protected under the Constitution, and the government employer may not unreasonably invade the employee's privacy. A government employee's locker, office, desk, or personal possessions are subject to search by a supervisor only where the employer has a factually-based reason to suspect that evidence of criminal conduct or of a violation of a workplace rule will be found in the employee's possessions. In other words, indiscriminate searches based on hunches, personal feelings, or little else are not allowed.

The fact that the post office department regulations indicated that lockers are subject to searches does not expand the post office's authority. A governmental entity cannot avoid constitutional limitations merely by claiming broader power than the Constitution authorizes.

I was just fired by a company for whom I worked the past six years. I was given no explanation, and I cannot figure out why they let me go. Can I be fired without cause?

A great myth has arisen in this country that people cannot be fired by their employers. Most Americans are employed in positions that do not require an employer to justify terminating employment. The only exceptions are when a union contract restricts management's right to fire an employee or when a contract exists between an employee and his employer for a definite period of time. Otherwise, your employment depends upon the mutual satisfaction of you and your employer.

The legal doctrine which regulates this type of employment is called "employment at will." At one time, it was said that an employee who served at the will of the employer could be discharged for good reason, for bad reason, or for no reason. Fortunately, the "employment at will" doctrine has been modified so that employees do have recourse for wrongful discharge under certain circumstances. Note the use of the term "certain circumstances."

Federal and state legislatures have limited an employer's unqualified right to discharge an employee by enacting legislation which prohibits termination of employment on certain grounds. Naturally, the federal law applies uniformly across the country, whereas the states have adopted a patchwork of different statutes limiting the "employment at will" doctrine. Consequently, some states provide much more protection for employees than do others. The legislative restrictions on "employment at will" tend to prohibit discharges which are based on discriminatory grounds such as race, gender, disability, age, religion, national origin, and, in some places, sexual preference. State laws are also likely to forbid terminations in retaliation for union organizing activities, or for filing sexual harassment, employment discrimination, or safety violation claims. Moreover, an employee's refusal to submit to sexual or romantic advances may not be the basis of discharge.

Greater protection for employees from wrongful termination, although again varying from state to state, has resulted from courts limiting "employment at will." The most significant protection has come from those state courts willing to find, in employer representations about job security, a limitation on "employment at will" that prevents an employer from firing an employee without cause. Courts have gone so far as to limit "employment at will" to situations where employers are acting fairly or in good faith. Obviously, the days of an employer's right to fire for good, bad, or no cause are over. How much protection you are afforded depends on the law of the particular state where you reside.

You can do some initial research on the subject at a public library, either in a book devoted to the law of employment practices in your state, or in a general book about employee protection. Don't forget to check on the statutes in your state, as well. If your termination resulted from discrimination which is barred by statute, a state or federal agency may exist which can initiate a complaint on your behalf. Alternatively, you may contact a lawyer in your area to learn about possible remedies. If you are going to sue for wrongful discharge, obviously, you will need a lawyer.

My employer has threatened to fire me for smoking—not even on the job, but at home. Is that fair?

Of course it's not fair, but that doesn't mean it can't be done.

Traditionally, what an American worker did at home, provided it was not against the law, was none of the boss's business. In fact, as a society, we may have only paid lip service to that maxim. There have always been Americans fired from their jobs because of political activism or civil rights activities, or an unconventional lifestyle lived away from and unconnected to the job. Rarely has there been much outcry over such terminations. Nonetheless, the myth persisted that what one does at home is not the boss's concern, so long as it does not affect behavior on the job.

Even aside from myths, however, employers today believe that some of an employee's outside activities do affect the workplace. There is a growing belief that an employee who smokes at home is likely to suffer from poor health and miss more work than a non-smoker, and use more health care services than a non-smoker, thus driving health insurance costs higher. These factors would tend to outweigh the employee's privacy claim, in a lawsuit over the employee's firing because of smoking.

Your employer has put the ball in your court. It seems you have the choice of your job or your smoking. At the very least, ask your employer to pay for a program to help you stop smoking.

10   ABORTION

Since slavery in the nineteenth century, no issue has so divided America as abortion. The polar extremes are irreconcilable, although most Americans seem to fall somewhere in the middle, favoring a woman's right to choose, tempered by reasonable state limitations on that choice. There seems to be little agreement as to what is a reasonable limitation. Nor is this an issue that is likely to go away. It appears destined to be litigated annually in the Supreme Court, and to be an issue in every presidential, congressional, and state gubernatorial and legislative election for years to come.

Well, does a woman have a right to an abortion?

Since 1973, the Constitution has guaranteed a woman's right to choose to terminate a pregnancy prior to the viability of the fetus. Since that year, there has been a steady erosion of the absoluteness of choice. In 1992, the Supreme Court narrowly affirmed the right to choose, but at the same time indicated a willingness to uphold substantial state regulation of that right.

Today in America, the right is grounded in the Constitution, but, in reality, may not exist for most women.

What types of conditions may be imposed by the state?

It should be understood that the conditions of access to an abortion, which are being adopted in many states, are aimed at dissuading women from choosing abortion and making it difficult to get an abortion. The Supreme Court is likely to uphold state restrictions, as long as they do not operate in a way likely to outlaw the procedure entirely for a group of women. For example, the Court has struck down state laws which require husband notification because it would prevent a group of women from exercising the right.

However, extensive state regulation effectively limiting a woman's right to choose has been upheld by the Supreme Court. A state may require a juvenile to notify her parents of her decision to have an abortion and obtain their permission, or seek a judge's permission, to proceed with the abortion without notifying the parents. The question arises whether such requirements actually promote family values, or simply work against juveniles who come from families where the ability to communicate is non-existent.

Other states require that women seeking abortions be advised of certain information, including the nature of an abortion procedure, the comparative risks of abortion and childbirth, and the probable development of the fetus. This information is an anti-choice lecture, designed to discourage women from having abortions. Furthermore, state mandatory waiting periods between the time of this "counseling" and the time when the procedure may be performed have been upheld.

I think I want to have an abortion, but have been unable to locate a place to have it in my community. What can I do?

For a great many women in America, legal abortions are no longer available. Eighty-three percent of American women reside in counties where hospitals will not do abortions and where there are no pre-term clinics. Nonetheless, there are places to turn. First, however, you should make the decision whether that is the proper course for you. Hopefully you won't have to make that decision by yourself, and there is a husband, lover, parent, friend, or counselor who will stand by you during this time and help you sort through your feelings. If you do make the decision to terminate your pregnancy, you must become familiar with the options and obstacles that await you.

If you have adequate funds, you can select locations where abortions are the most accessible and the least restricted. Obviously, the unavailability of local abortions adversely affects poor women the most. These women often must travel some distance to secure an abortion. In addition, in many states, these women now face mandatory waiting periods between the time they first seek an abortion, have the required anti-choice lecture, and then may have the abortion performed. Either the woman finds money to pay for the abortion and a hotel, or else she must travel home, sometimes a considerable distance, and then return for the abortion after the mandated delay.

Legal abortions are virtually inaccessible to poor women for other reasons, as well. Thirty states will not provide Medicaid funding for abortions, unless the woman's life is in danger, and another eight will provide public funding only if the pregnancy resulted from rape or incest or the woman's life is in danger. President Clinton lifted the federal government's "gag rule," which prohibited doctors and counsellors at federally funded family planning clinics from discussing abortion as an option, even when a patient initiated the discussion or requested information. Now that information is available at federally funded clinics.

Whether you are able to pay for your abortion, if you have made the decision to terminate your pregnancy, you should contact one of the national organizations through its (800) telephone number, for information about the options available to you. Planned Parenthood will provide the number of the affiliate closest to you. Planned Parenthood's toll free number is 1(800) 829-7732. If you are located a considerable distance from the affiliate, the affiliate is obligated to tell you about three alternative facilities that you can contact. The affiliate, also, will be able to tell you about the legal restrictions which exist in your state.

INDEX

Cross references to another main heading are in CAPITAL LETTERS.

ABORTIONS, 149-151
"Gag rule", 151
Husband, notification, 149
Information given to woman, 150, 151
Juvenile, parental notification, 150
Locating place for, 150-151
Planned Parenthood, 151
Right to, 149
State limitations, 149-150
Waiting period, 150-151

ACCIDENTS—See CARS.

AIDS
Anonymous testing, 107-110
Hotline, 110

AID TO DEPENDENT CHILDREN
Home visits to determine eligibility, 71-72

AIRPORTS, 35-47
Drug courier profile, 38-39
Drug enforcement stops, 38-45
  Officer identification, 43-44
  Prohibited actions by law enforcement officers, 39-42
Identification check of officer, 43-44
Ignoring officer, 43
Illegal stops, significance, 41-42
Jurisdiction of law enforcement agencies, 38
Luggage search, consent to, 39-45
Luggage X-ray equipment, 36-38
Magnetometers, 36-38
Passenger tickets
  Dishonoring of, 45-47

AIRPORTS—*continued*
Passenger tickets—*continued*
  Federal Aviation Agency regulations governing, 46-47
  Stolen tickets, 46-47
  Using another person's, 45-47
Refusal to allow search, 37-38
Security checkpoints, 36-38
Security, stopped by, 42-45
Weapons searches, 37-38

ALCOHOL, DRIVING UNDER INFLUENCE OF—See
    DRUNK DRIVING.

ARRESTS, 111-128
    See also JAILS.
Attorney, prisoner selection of, 122-124
Bail, 113-115
Booking, 112-113
Bus travel, 49-50
Computerized records of, 112-113
Conversations with officers, 117-122
Definition, 111-112
Domestic violence, 67-68
Drinking, underage; officer sighting when called on another
    matter, 65-66
Drunk driving, 26
False arrest, bus search, refusal to cooperate, 49-50
Felony, bail, 115
Good will of officers, 120
Lawyer, prisoner selection of, 122-124
Miranda rights, 117-122
Misdemeanor, bail, 114
Opportunity to request assistance, 115-117
Prisoner right to representation, 120-122
Residential, 64-67
Silent, remaining, 118-122
"Station house bail", 114
Telephone calls, 115-117
Warrantless entry of residence, 64-67

ATTORNEYS—See LAWYERS.

AUDITORIUMS
Pat-down search before entering, 93-95

AUTOMOBILES—See CARS.

"BIG BROTHER"
Governmental access to personal information, 54-55

BRIBERY
Police officer, during traffic stop, 12-13

BUILDING INSPECTORS
Residential quarters, entry, 70-71

BUS TRAVEL, 47-51
Arrests, 49-50
Author's encounter with authority, 1-2
Delaying departure, 51
False arrest liability of officer, 49-50
Forcing passenger off bus, 49-50
Luggage searches, 47-51
Refusal to cooperate with officers, 48-50
Right to leave bus, 48
Unreasonable delay, 51
"Working the buses", 47

CARS, 7-33
        See also TRAFFIC STOPS.
Accidents, 30-33
   Driver responsibilities, 30-32
   Police reports following, 31
   Precautions following, 31-32
   Vehicle belonging to another person, 32-33
   Vehicle lent to another licensed driver, 32-33
Drunk driving—See DRUNK DRIVING.
Impounding of vehicle, 15-16, 22-24
Safety inspection checkpoints, 30
Searches—See TRAFFIC STOPS, at Vehicle searches.
Sobriety checkpoints, 27-30
Towed vehicles, 22-24
   Inventory of contents, 23
Traffic stops—See TRAFFIC STOPS.

COLLEGES AND UNIVERSITIES, 77-110
Academic competence, court review, 90-91
Administration as landlord, 78
AIDS testing, anonymous, 107-110
Athletes, drug testing, 95-96
Auditoriums, pat-down and visual searches, 93-95

COLLEGES AND UNIVERSITIES—*continued*
Campus police, authority, 91-95
Date rape, 104-107
Disciplinary action, 83-86
  Off-campus infractions, 89-90
Disorderly conduct, 91-93
Dormitories—See Residence halls, this heading.
Drinking rules of college, enforcement at sorority and frater-
    nity parties, 82
Drug testing, 95-96
  Athletes, 95-96
Duty to protect students, employees, and visitors, 103-104
Enforcement of rules and regulations, 82
Evidence obtained in illegal search, use, 84-85
Fellowship, effect on income tax, 131
Flunking out, court review, 90-91
Harrassment, sexual, 97-99
HIV testing, anonymous, 107-110
Immunity from damages, 103-104
Landlord-tenant relationship of administration and students,
    78
Liability, victims of crime, 103-104
Misdemeanors committed by students, 87-90
Negligence, 103-104
Off-campus activities, 87-90
Parties, enforcement of college rules and regulations, 82
Pat-down searches, 93-95
Police involvement in disciplinary matters, 85-86
Police searches of student rooms, 81
Pranks, 87-90
Records, students; disclosure of information, 96-97
Residence halls
  Evidence, college turning over to police, 85-86
  Illegal search, use of evidence at disciplinary hearing, 84-85
  Police, entry into dorm room, 81
  Residence assistants, entry into dorm room, 77-81
    Illegal search, use of evidence at disciplinary hearing, 84-
    85
Scholarship, effect on income tax, 131
Searches of student rooms, 77-81
  Evidence, college turning over to police, 85-86
  Illegal search, use of evidence at disciplinary hearing, 84-85
Security of campus and buildings, 103-104
Sexual assaults, 104-107
Sexual harassment, 97-99

COLLEGES AND UNIVERSITIES—*continued*
Stadiums, pat-down and visual searches, 93-95
Student identification cards, loan to another student, 86-87
Student records, disclosure of information, 96-97
Theft of student property, 102-104
Tuition reduction, effect on income tax, 131
Visual searches, 93-95

CONCERTS
Pat-down search, 93-95

CREDIT, 133-140
Cards
   Annual fees, 134-136
   Guarantor requirements, 133-134
   Inappropriate use, 136-138
   Interest charges, 134-136, 136-138
   Issuers, evaluation, 134-136
   Merchants, charges on, 135
   Overspending, 136-138
   Terms and conditions, 135-136
   Unpaid balances, 135
Developing a credit history, 133-134
Errors on credit reports, 138-139
Loans, 138-139
Ratings, 139-140
Reporting agencies, 138-139
Reports, 138-139
   Free, 139-140

CRIMES
Arrests—See ARRESTS.
Campus, on, 102-104
Domestic violence, 66-69
Drunk driving—See DRUNK DRIVING.
Obscene phone calls, 99-100
Sexual assault, 104-107
Sexual harassment, 97-99
Trespass, 100-102

DATE RAPE, 104-106

DOMESTIC VIOLENCE
Police responsibilities and right of entry, 66-69

DORMITORIES—See COLLEGES AND UNIVERSITIES,
     at Residence halls.

DRIVERS' LICENSES
Airports, officer's request to show license, 39-42
License checkpoints, 30
Traffic stop, officer's request to show license, 13-17
  Expired license, 15
  Suspended license, 16
  Unlicensed driver, 16

DRIVING UNDER THE INFLUENCE—See DRUNK
     DRIVING.

DRUGS
Airports, search for—See AIRPORTS, generally.
Buses, search for—See BUS TRAVEL, generally.
Cars, search for—See TRAFFIC STOPS, at Vehicle searches.
Driving under influence of—See DRUNK DRIVING,
        generally.
Testing—See DRUG TESTING.

DRUG TESTING
Athletes at college, 95-96
Colleges, 95-96
Employees, 142-143

DRUNK DRIVING
Arrests, 26
Breath tests
  Attorney, consulting before taking, 27
  Refusal to take, 26-27
Checkpoint stops, 27-30
Job application, disclosure of conviction, 141-142
Roadside tests
  Attorney, consulting before taking, 27
  Refusal to take, 26-27
Traffic stops, 24-27
Video recording after stop, 26-27

EMPLOYMENT, 141-147
     See also JOBS.

FALSE ARREST
Bus search, refusal to cooperate, 49-50

FEDERAL AVIATION AGENCY
Passenger manifest requirement, 46-47

FEDERAL INCOME TAX—See TAXES.

FELLOWSHIPS
Income tax, effect, 131

FIGHTS, 66-69

FRATERNITY PARTIES
Drinking rules of college, enforcement, 82

HARASSMENT
Intruders, by, 100-102
Sexual, colleges and universities, 97-99
Telephone, by, 99-100, 100-102
Trespassers, 100-102

HIGH SCHOOLS
Locker searches, 82-83

HIV
Testing, anonymous, 107-110

HOME—See RESIDENTIAL QUARTERS.

INCOME TAXES—See TAXES.

JAILS—See also ARRESTS, generally.
Avoiding being held, 113-115
Conversations with other prisoners, 126-127
Pre-trial incarceration, 126
   Release, 127-128

JOBS, 141-147
Crimes, disclosure, 141-142
Desk, search of, 143-144
Drug testing, 142-143
Drunk driving conviction, disclosure, 141-142
"Employment at will", 144-146
Firing
   Employer's rights, 144-45
   Smoking, 146-147
Locker searches, 143-144
Possessions, search of, 143-144

JOBS—*continued*
Search of desk, locker, or personal possessions, 143-144
Smoking, firing due to, 146-147

LANDLORD AND TENANT
Eviction of tenant, 73-75
Landlord rights, 57-58
Tenant rights, 73-75

LAWYERS
Appointment of, 125
Drunk driving stop, consulting prior to taking tests, 27
Evaluation of, 122-124
Prisoner right to representation, 120-122
Prisoner selection of, 122-124
Responsibilities to client, 128
Selection of, 122-124

LOANS, 138-139

LOCKERS
Employee's locker, search, 143-144
Student's locker, search, 82-83

MAGNETOMETERS, 36-38

MASTERCARD—See CREDIT, at Cards, generally.

MINORS
Abortion, parental notification, 150
Students—See COLLEGES AND UNIVERSITIES, generally;
        STUDENTS.

MIRANDA RIGHTS, 117-122

MOTOR VEHICLES—See CARS.

NOISE COMPLAINTS, 63-67

NOISY PARTIES, 63-65

PARTIES
College drinking rules, enforcement, 82
Noise complaints, 63-65

PERSONAL INFORMATION
Access to records, 54-55
College student records, disclosure of information, 96-97

PERSONAL SAFETY
Residential quarters, 100-102

PLANNED PARENTHOOD
Abortion information, providing, 151

RAPE, 104-107

RECORDS
Access to records, 54-55
College student records, disclosure of information, 96-97

RENTERS—See LANDLORD AND TENANT.

RESIDENCE HALLS—See COLLEGES AND
        UNIVERSITIES.

RESIDENTIAL QUARTERS, 53-81, 84-86
ADC, home visits to determine eligibility, 71-72
Building inspectors, 70-71
    Warrants to enter premises, 71
Child welfare investigators, 72-73
Colleges—See COLLEGES AND UNIVERSITIES, at Resi-
        dence halls.
Domestic violence, 66-69
Entry to arrest, 64-67
Fights, 66-69
Landlord rights, 57-58
911 calls
    Police right of entry, 66-67
Noisy parties, 63-65
Parents granting permission to search, 59-60
Personal safety, 100-102
Police entry, 55-68
    Consent, 55-59
    Warrants, 56
Precautions, minimal, 53
Roommates granting permission to search, 58-59
Searches, 55-66
    Uninvited entry by officer, 64-67
    Inventory of items seized, 61
    Limits imposed by warrants, 60-62

RESIDENTIAL QUARTERS—*continued*
Searches—*continued*
  Nighttime searches, 61
  Probable cause, 63
  Warrantless, 62-63
  Warrants, scope of authority to search, 60-61
  Yards, 61-62
Tenant rights, 57-58
Trespass, 58
Universities—See COLLEGES AND UNIVERSITIES, at
     Residence halls.
Yards, 61-62

SCHOLARSHIPS
Income tax, effect, 131

SCHOOLS
Locker searches, 82-83

SEARCHES
Airports—See AIRPORTS, generally.
Buses—See BUS TRAVEL, generally.
Cars—See TRAFFIC STOPS, at Vehicle searches.
Employee's desk, locker, or personal possessions, 143-144
Home—See RESIDENTIAL QUARTERS, at Searches.
Inventory of items seized, 61
Limits imposed by warrants, 60-62
Narrative of encounter, importance of writing, 6
  Airports, encounter in, 44
  Car searches, 22
Warrants, scope of authority to search, 60-62

SEXUAL ASSAULT, 104-107

SEXUAL HARASSMENT, 97-99

SMOKING
Firing of employee due to, 146-147

SOBRIETY CHECKPOINTS, 27-30

SOCIAL SERVICES WORKERS
Child welfare investigators, home visits by, 72-73
Home visits, rights of residents, 71-73

SORORITY PARTIES
Drinking rules of college, enforcement, 82

STADIUMS
Pat-down search, 93-95

STATE INCOME TAX—See TAXES.

STUDENTS—See also COLLEGES AND UNIVERSITIES,
    generally.
Locker searches, 82-83
Records, disclosure of information, 96-97
Taxes
   Interest income, 130
   Payroll deductions, 129-130
   Refunds, 129-130

TAXES, 129-132
Dependent students, payroll deductions, 129-130
Educational assistance, 131
Fellowships, 131
Filing status, 130-131
Interest income, 130
Refunds, dependent students, 129-130
Returns
   Extension of time, 131
   Filing status, 130-131
Scholarships, 131
Tuition reduction, 131
Withholding, inadequate, 130-131

TENANTS—See LANDLORD AND TENANT.

THEFT
Student property on campus, 102-104

TRAFFIC STOPS, 7-33
Behavior of motorist, 8-11
Bribery of officer, 12-13
Courtesy, 9
Crime evidence found as result of illegal stop, 7-8
Delay between stop and approach of officer, 11
Driver identification requests, 13-17
   Expired license, 15
   Failure to produce license, 13-17
   Lack of operator's license, 16

TRAFFIC STOPS—*continued*
Driver identification requests—*continued*
  Suspended license, 16
Driver, search of, 11-12
Drunk driving—See DRUNK DRIVING.
Exiting vehicle
  Motorist's initiative, 10-11
  Officer's order, 11-12
Fleeing officer, 8
Illegal stops, 7-8
Impaired driving—See DRUNK DRIVING.
Impounding of vehicle, 15-16, 22-24
Incriminating evidence in plain sight, 12
License checkpoints, 30
License plate check, 11
Plainclothes officer, by, 9-10
Reason for stop necessary, 7
Rudeness, avoidance, 9
Sobriety checkpoints, 27-30
Unmarked police car, by, 9-10
Vehicle checkpoints, 30
Vehicle registration requests, 13-17
  Failure to produce registration, 13-14
Vehicle searches, 11-12, 17-22
  Illegal searches, 18
  Legal searches, 19-22
  Refusal of consent, right to, 17-19
  Towed vehicles, 23-24
  Unreasonable searches, 21-22
  Warrantless searches, 19-22
  Whole vehicle searches, 21-22
Weapon in plain sight, 12

TRAFFIC TICKETS—See also TRAFFIC STOPS, generally.
Arrest booking, computer check bringing up, 112
Talking officer out of issuing, 12-13

TRAVEL—See AIRPORTS; BUS TRAVEL; CARS; TRAF-
    FIC STOPS.

TUITION ASSISTANCE
Income tax, effect, 131

UNIVERSITIES—See COLLEGES AND UNIVERSITIES.

VEHICLES—See CARS; TRAFFIC STOPS.

VIDEO RECORDING
Drunk driver, 26-27

VISA CREDIT CARD—See CREDIT, at Cards, generally.

WARRANTS
Building inspectors, right of entry, 70-71
Home, search warrant; scope of authority to search, 60-61

WELFARE
ADC, home visits to determine eligibility, 71-72